# The Science of Takedowns, Throws and Grappling for Self-defense

# The Science of Takedowns, Throws and Grappling for Self-defense

by
Martina Sprague

Turtle Press                    Hartford

To contact the author or to order additional copies of this book:
Turtle Press
P.O. Box 290206
Wethersfield, CT 06129-0206
1-800-778-8785

ISBN 1-880336-80-4
LCCN 2003001360

Printed in the United States of America

10 9 8 7 6 5 4 3 2 1

**Library of Congress Cataloging-in-Publication Data**

Sprague, Martina.
  The science of takedowns, throws, and grappling for self-defense / by
Martina Sprague.
      p. cm.
Includes index.
  ISBN 1-880336-80-4 (pbk.)
  1. Self-defense. 2. Equilibrium. I. Title.
GV1111 .S735 2003
613.6'6—dc21
                                    2003001360

# Contents

*To the memory of Per-Åke Lax, my wonderful
big brother and best childhood friend.*

## **Acknowledgements**

Many thanks to my friends (listed alphabetically), who took time from their busy schedules to pose for photos:
Per-Åke Lax, chapter 2
Keith Livingston, chapters 5, 6, 9, and 10
Mark Livingston, chapters 5, 6, 9, and 10
Tom Sprague, chapters 1, 7, and 8
Wm. David Swisher, introduction and chapters 11, 12, and 13
Dave Teachout, chapters 3 and 4
Len Tomei, chapters 12 and 13
Alex Wilsher, introduction and chapters 11, 12, and 13
Also, thanks to Cynthia Kim and Turtle Press for the hard work, many helpful suggestions, and beautiful design of the book and cover.

# Foreword

*by Sergeant Keith R. Livingston*
*South Salt Lake Police Department*

We often think of a concept as merely a thought or an idea. But for the purpose of martial arts, a concept is the idea behind the technique. In a broader sense, concepts can bridge from one technique to another. For example, hip rotation is a concept that we find in a hundred techniques, so mastery of the concept becomes as important as mastery of each individual technique.

We have learned through experience that during a critical incident involving combat, fine motor skills tend to fail. However, broader conceptual thinking has a high success rate. One of my favorite examples is the concept of inherent weakness, which says that all persons have the same weak points on their bodies. You cannot strengthen your eyeballs, eardrums, nose, or testicles. When faced with life or death, the concept of inherent weakness can be employed by attacking these targets relentlessly with any tools or techniques you have available. Conceptual thinking is usually more successful than confining yourself to a specific set of predetermined moves.

Conceptual thinking has also brought much success in the area of takedowns. As a police officer and arrest and control instructor, I have developed the basic premise that if the violator is non-compliant and combative, our first course of action is to remove him from his feet. I have found unbalancing techniques to be highly successful regardless of size, sex, or level of fitness. After I conclude the technique training, I teach two valuable concepts:

1. Where the head goes, the body will follow.
2. Direct all energy toward the goal.

Both of these concepts tend to achieve the same goal of getting the opponent on the ground. I end the lesson with this advice: *When the technique is failing, remember the concept. The concept will likely fix the technique.* I will leave you with the following real-life example:

I recently taught an eight-hour seminar on takedowns. Throughout the day, we spent several hours practicing takedown techniques. The final ninety minutes of the seminar were devoted entirely to exploring the *technique behind the technique*. I showed the class that by controlling their opponent's head, they could move the heavier body anywhere they wanted it to go. I showed them that if their goal was to take an adversary down, then all energy must be directed toward the ground. Finally, I showed them the concepts of stealing a person's balance. I left the class with the following advice: *Until you have had adequate time to practice the technique, dwell on the concepts that make it work.*

A few weeks later, I received a phone call from a police officer that had attended my seminar. He told me that my advice had saved his life. He proceeded to relate how, two days after attending the seminar, he was working the midnight shift. He confessed that he hadn't had time to practice the techniques, but that he had thought considerably about the concepts. At approximately one o'clock in the morning, he and a back-up unit were dispatched to a physically violent domestic dispute. When they arrived, the front door was ajar. They could hear a female screaming while a male was beating her. As soon as they made entry, the male turned and rushed the officer relating this story. The officer braced himself for impact and a standing struggle ensued, with the man trying to remove the officer's weapon. Not able to reach the weapon himself, the officer grabbed the man's head and, with all the focus and direction of energy he could muster, successfully threw the man to the ground. While the man was still stunned, the officer stood, drew his weapon, and ordered the man to lie still while the back-up unit handcuffed him.

It is success stories like these that place such great importance on conceptual learning. Concepts always have correlation from one technique to another, and will bring greater proficiency to all techniques.

# Overview of Concepts

The primary intent of this book is to study the principles of takedowns for the purpose of self-defense. A takedown or throw requires the ability to disturb your opponent's balance. When we first start out with takedowns, we have a tendency to try to out-muscle, or force, our adversary down. Naturally, the stronger or bigger person will win, making takedown practice discouraging for the lighter weight student. However, a successfully executed takedown relies only on one scientific principle: the location of the center of gravity. The focus of this book is how to disturb an adversary's center of gravity while retaining your own; in short, how to get your opponent on the ground without going down with him. Because the principle used for shifting the center of gravity is identical for small, big, friendly, or mean people, understanding this principle allows a smaller person to take a larger adversary down with relative ease. The book's primary aim of discussing principles, rather than specific techniques, makes it adaptable to almost any situation where a takedown is warranted.

Both takedowns and throws accomplish the same thing: to get your opponent on the ground. However, although a throw is often more dynamic than a takedown, it is also more difficult for a lighter person to pull off against a bigger adversary. Furthermore, throws don't work if you don't have a solid foundation. The same is not true for takedowns. If your opponent lifts you off your feet, you can still use the principle of balance manipulation to take him down. To make the text easily applicable to a self-defense situation, we will focus on takedowns first. Once you master the takedown, it is relatively easy to adapt your positioning slightly, and use the same principles to execute a throw. Many of the principles discussed in this book can also be used as "rescue techniques" when coming to the aid of another person. When you have learned how to successfully unbalance an adversary, a variety of effective and easy to use presses will be discussed, giving you the option to subdue him on the ground until help arrives.

We will mainly explore techniques that focus on gross motor skills. This enables you to use the information under stressful conditions with minimal amount of training. However, it is essential that you do practice the concepts discussed in the book. A number of exercises have been included for this purpose. Perhaps the most important principle is developing the right mind-set about a high threat street encounter. It is easy to talk about how one *should* think, or how one *should* react, or what one *should* do, but it is realistic practice that brings insight. Takedowns, throws, and presses all require close physical contact with your opponent. This, in itself, may be an uncomfortable experience for those not trained in the martial arts. It is therefore recommended that, at first, you practice physical closeness with a person you trust (but not necessarily know well), and that you really think about and allow these issues to play themselves out in your mind.

To say that one should not show fear when faced with a threat is ideal but unrealistic. It is okay to feel fear, even show it, but it is not okay to give in to it and letting it paralyze you. Nor should you be afraid of your own abilities. Thinking that because of your background and training you are a dangerous person, who must use his "powers" with caution, is equally unrealistic. There are few mysteries in martial arts, and many highly trained martial artists don't fare well in a street encounter. But this does not mean that there is something wrong with the art or the principles. Rather, it falls back on how the person has trained for the encounter. If you train all your life with no or little actual contact, it is not likely that you can suddenly bring out your powers when it counts. In training, do not pair up only with those you like, or only with your friends, or women only with women, etc. The more uncomfortable you are with your training partners, the more beneficial training can be, as long as it is supervised and ethical. Get used to the physical closeness of another person, and if he stinks from a hangover from last night, so much the better.

You can practice techniques to death, but if you don't have the clarity of mind, or the courage to use them in a real encounter, all your training is useless. The greatest disservice you can do yourself is to practice the techniques with no or minimal contact. I'm not saying that you should get into a real battle in order to learn how to get out of one; I'm saying that you must get banged around at least a little in order to learn to use your skills in real time. This is why your mind-set should be an offensive one. The idea of taking your adversary down without hurting him, so that you can run to safety, is noble. But how does one know exactly how far to go when one's life is at stake? Be prepared to do whatever necessary to save your own life, with minimal injury to yourself or your loved ones. You have a right to continue until *you* no longer perceive a threat, and you are the ultimate authority on when that is. In training, you don't train with the intent of hurting your partner, but you do train with intensity and seriousness. You must show courage and a will to learn, and train with a variety of partners, preferably those bigger, stronger, faster, and more daring than you. When you give your practice partner, or your opponent, all the physical benefits, you must use correct principle in order to be effective. A big and strong person can always use his size and strength against a weaker person, so the equalizer comes in skill and mind-set.

My intent is not to show you every technique that can be used for self-defense. Although strikes and kicks are valuable self-defense tools that we will touch on, they are not the focus of this book. Even if you are a good puncher or kicker, if your weight is considerably less than your opponent's, it is difficult to generate the momentum needed to execute a strike powerful enough to end a confrontation against a person intent on hurting you. Most people can take a few good blows without it stopping them. Those who do stop when hit usually have a psychological disadvantage; they have never been hit before and think that they are hurt worse than they are. But these kinds of people are not likely to initiate an attack on you in the first place. A strike or kick that lands precisely on an inherently weak area of your opponent's anatomy may well do enough damage to end the fight. But it is my belief that the time and adrenaline constraints of a real confrontation make it difficult to execute or rely on such a blow. If your first strike fails to be effective, and the distance between you and your opponent is such that he can grab you, further strikes may be difficult to execute. Takedowns and throws lend themselves to this fighting range. We will talk about strikes and kicks as softening techniques, but will not spend a great deal of time discussing how to execute or develop powerful strikes. If you can strike or kick and get away, or finish your opponent with a good blow without clinching, by all means . . . Whatever gets you to safety is the right move. However, unbalancing moves give you an *option* every time there is body contact.

Throughout your study, we will emphasize correct principle coupled with correct mind-set (or correct thinking). Although the possible attacks are many and only limited by the attacker's imagination, the principles are few and can be counted on the fingers of one hand. Why train in principles rather than in techniques? A specific technique works only for a specific situation. Training in, and building an arsenal of, techniques assumes that you know beforehand what type of attack that is coming, or that you have enough techniques memorized and perfected that you are prepared for every type of attack with every slight variation. However, unless you have had time to practice these techniques so that they are muscle memory, you are not likely to be able to pull them out and use them in the time available in a chaotic situation. Focusing on learning principles has a great advantage, because it eliminates the need to remember a hundred specific defenses for a hundred specific attacks.

A principle is a little broader in scope than a technique, and can involve such things as position of superiority and direction. For example, we can say that any time you have established a superior position slightly toward your opponent's back, you can use a neck takedown that involves shifting the center of gravity to the rear by cupping your opponent's chin, tilting his head back, and directing your energy toward the ground, allowing gravity to take its course. Or we can say that any time you are attacked in such a manner that you have access to your opponent's centerline (round house punch or kick, wide slashing knife attack, wide swing with a club, etc.), you can use an unbalancing move that involves shifting his foundation away from his upper body center of gravity by ducking the strike, grabbing his leg, and using it as a lever to throw him off balance. Having knowledge of the principles and motions of possible types of attacks enables you to prepare both physically and mentally for the encounter.

Because the principles discussed in this book are scientifically based, if you study and practice these principles, you will have a clear advantage over the larger adversary, or the "bully" of the street, who is not familiar with the scientific side of takedowns. Takedowns and throws rely not on strength, but on leverage and movement based around one's center of gravity, and are therefore well suited for smaller or weaker people. If you happen to be of small stature, try to see it as an advantage during the course of your training, as being small forces you to rely on the principles of physics rather than on your strength. Once you know how to do this, you will gain confidence in your abilities and be able to apply these principles to a myriad of different scenarios. The principles we will use are:

1. Shifting the center of gravity
2. Position of superiority
3. The use of straight and linear momentum
4. The use of torque
5. Establishing and maintaining an aggressive mind-set

Correct use of these principles helps you unbalance an adversary in both standing and grappling situations involving the following scenarios:

1. Striking attacks, where your opponent punches or kicks you (including knife and stick attacks)
2. Grabbing attacks, where your opponent tries to hurt you, pull you along with him, or force you off balance
3. Surprise attacks, where you are attacked from behind, or where your opponent uses his momentum to rush you
4. Attacks initiated by you, either because you sense a threat that you try to keep from developing, or because there is a need to come to the rescue of another person

When training in throws and takedowns, mats should be used to protect against injuries due to falling. It is also a good idea to have basic knowledge of how to fall in order to spread the force of impact over the body to lessen its effect. Refer to the safety tips on the next page for tips on falling. You will see additional safety reminders throughout the text.

When taken down or thrown on rough or hard surfaces, the force and risk of injury is much more severe, due to the lack of protective mats. The element of surprise also precludes the assailant from breaking the fall. An added benefit is that impact with the ground will at least stun him long enough to give you the time advantage you need to escape or further subdue him on the ground.

Throughout your study, keep in mind that your primary objective is to unbalance your opponent, thereby creating an opportunity for you to flee to safety. Your secondary objective is to subdue him on the ground until help arrives, but this will only be done if your unbalancing move fails to ensure your or a loved one's safety.

## Safety Tips

1. When learning to fall, start by practicing from your knees. Use mats to cushion the fall, or fall from a standing position and onto a bed.

2. Tuck your chin down toward your chest to avoid bouncing your head against the ground. If the fall is frontal, catch yourself on your forearms (not your hands, wrists, elbows, or knees).

3. Spread your weight as much as possible to break the fall and avoid injury to joints or other sensitive body parts. Use headgear and elbow pads for extra protection.

4. Communicate with your partner. Ask him or her to help you slow the fall until you get proficient at falling.

5. Discuss the technique with your partner prior to executing it. Horse-play or surprise attacks in training can easily lead to injury.

The following section is provided to forewarn you of the concepts you will use during training. Studying and thinking about these concepts beforehand helps you relate to them when they recur in the text later, with the result of speeding up the learning process. The concepts are listed in alphabetical order with a reference for further learning. Read them all before commencing your study, and refer to them as often as necessary during the course of your training.

# Explanation of Concepts

### ATTACK LINE

The attack line is created by linear movement between you and your opponent, and allows your opponent to attack more effectively. When faced with an aggressor, stay slightly to one side of the attack line, move back and forth across the attack line, or employ circular motion to thwart his attack. If you have the opportunity to initiate the move and use your momentum to knock your opponent off balance, try to stay on the attack line in order to focus your power in the direction of your attack. This does not mean that you have to operate along your opponent's centerline; only that you should move linearly and in the direction of power.

**Positioning Preparatory To The Takedown, Chapter 2.**

### CENTERLINE

The centerline is an imaginary line approximately five inches wide, running vertically on the front or back of your body. Striking the targets found on the centerline (nose, jaw, throat, heart, solar plexus, groin, base of neck, spine, and tailbone) is likely to cause serious injury or death. The centerline is also where your strength is focused. Any time a technique is not lined up with your centerline, power loss occurs. The closer you can keep your techniques to your centerline, the more powerful and effortless they will be.

**Finger Locks, Chapter 11.**

**Most frontal attacks are aimed at your centerline. Be aware!**

## CENTER OF GRAVITY

This is your balance point. Any time your center of gravity does not fall above your foundation, you will lose balance. Understanding this principle enables you to unbalance a much stronger, bigger, or more aggressive adversary. When a person's center of gravity is manipulated, he is unable to utilize his strength effectively. By understanding how the human body works, you can manipulate its many natural bends and balance points to take your adversary down.

**Defining Balance, Chapter 1.**

## COMBINATIONS

Whenever possible, attack in combinations. One strike or defensive move and counter-attack are not likely to end the fight. Think beyond the first move. When practicing unbalancing techniques, a combination should be thought of as any set of moves that places you closer to your objective. A combination could be comprised of a set-up or distraction, a gap closure, a softening technique, an unbalancing technique, and a finishing technique.

**Softening Techniques, Chapter 2.**

## COMPLETION OF MOTION

Any started motion must come to completion before you can reset your body's balance. For example, if your opponent raises one foot off the ground to take a step forward, he is in a "balance inferior" position until he has again replanted that foot. This is a window of opportunity for you to move in with a takedown.

**Defining Balance, Chapter 1.**

## DETERMINATION

Your determination may be the deciding factor between success and failure. Getting caught up in emotions and fears inhibits your ability to respond to a threat. With practice and increased confidence come determination and the ability to face a situation and follow through to a logical conclusion. An aggressive mind-set will more often than not help save your life.

**On The Chaos Of An Attack, Chapter 13.**

## DIRECTION OF ENERGY

If your goal is to take your adversary down, you must direct all your energy toward the ground. If your goal is to use body momentum to knock your opponent off balance, you must direct all your energy along the attack line. Power is derived from several sources working in harmony toward a common goal. Balance is an element of power. You must center your upper body over the foundation of your lower body and project all energy in the same direction. Power loss most often results from opposing movements in body mechanics.

**Direction Of Energy, Chapter 3.**

## ECONOMY OF MOTION

In a high threat situation, it is imperative that you gain control and end the fight as quickly as possible. Use techniques that will do the most amount of damage in the fewest number of moves. When you waste time, you allow your opponent additional time, giving him a position of strength. A low kick, for example, may be more economical than a high kick, because it is closer to the target and requires less agility to perform. A neck manipulation takedown may be more economical than a wrist lock, because it requires less fine motor skills, and can be done through linear movement.

**How To Practice Your Art, Chapter 11.**

## ENVIRONMENT AWARENESS

Use the environment to your advantage. Try to get something between yourself and the attacker. An obstacle can be used to unbalance your opponent or bar further aggressiveness. Don't go empty handed against an armed attacker. Find something in the environment that can be used as a weapon. Be aware of escape routes and objects that may obscure your vision. Be thoroughly familiar with your most frequently visited environment (your home).

**Awareness Exercise, Chapter 2.**

## ESCALATION OF FORCE

Start with the least amount of force necessary to control the threat. Try to recognize and remove yourself from a dangerous situation before it requires you to take action. If action has to be taken, try to de-escalate the situation. In a verbal confrontation, this may simply involve talking to your opponent and resolving the issue without physical contact. If your opponent approaches you, don't wait until it is too late to turn the situation to your advantage. When you decide to go ahead with your unbalancing move, you must pursue it with full force and intent. How far you go after you have taken your opponent down depends on the situation, your ability to get away, and the perceived threat. Never assume that a fight is over because you nailed your opponent with one good strike, unbalancing move, or joint break. We are driven by our mental determination, and many times when a fight *should* have ended, it might not because of added adrenaline. Once you decide to let go of your adversary, know that the threat may not be over. Consider how to reapply control or continue with a second unbalancing technique. You may need to escalate the force to a press and breaking technique against a joint or, if it is a matter of life or death, take a more lethal approach.

**Is It Ethical To Kill In Self-Defense, Chapter 13.**

Don't assume that a fight is over because you landed a good strike. Finishing with an unbalancing move may buy you time to get to safety.

## EXHAUSTING THE MOTION

For a technique to be effective, you must take it to completion. When you have nothing left to drive forward with, the motion of the technique is said to have exhausted itself. For example, if you are attempting to push your opponent away but are unable to take a step forward, the only way you can push is by starting with bent arms and gradually straightening your arms. Once your arms are straight, the motion of the technique is exhausted, unless you can also step forward and keep pushing. When engaged in a confrontation that involves movement of mass, like a takedown or a grappling situation, be careful not to place yourself in a position that exhausts the motion of your technique. One way to avoid this is by keeping your opponent's center of mass close to your own center of mass, and relying on movement in your body to unbalance him, rather than on movement in your arms alone.

**Full Nelson From The Front, Chapter 6.**

## FINE VS. GROSS MOTOR SKILLS

Fine motor skills involve the use of precise hand/eye coordination, whereas gross motor skills involve the use of larger muscle groups. Because of the way the nervous system works, you are physically stronger and faster when under stress, than you are in a low stress situation. However, you are also mentally weaker and unable to use precision or solve complicated problems. Gross motor skills are therefore more stress compatible than fine motor skills, which is something you should keep in mind when training for self-defense.

**Attacking Your Opponent's Arms, Chapter 5.**

**If a wrist control hold involving fine motor skills fails, can you reverse direction and gain outside superiority for an unbalancing move against the elbow?**

## FIRST TOUCH

Use the moment of first touch as a cue to explode forward with a takedown. The moment you first make physical contact with your opponent, regardless of who initiates the attack, is your window of opportunity. Physical contact has a tendency to momentarily freeze your opponent or halt his advance. As long as you are aware of this, you can work to eliminate your own tendency to freeze.

**Momentum And First Touch, Chapter 3.**

## FOOTWORK

Footwork can be used to create a gap or close distance. Perhaps the most important aspect of footwork is your ability to deceive your opponent. By constantly moving and switching direction, your opponent will have difficulty determining when within range to attack. Use footwork to gain a window of opportunity for your unbalancing move.

**Defining Balance, Chapter 1.**

## FREEZING

When you freeze your opponent, you momentarily inhibit his ability to respond. You may be able to freeze your opponent's advance through a distraction or the concept of first touch. The moment you make contact with any part of his body is a signal to move ahead with your unbalancing technique. When touching or slapping your opponent, his mind momentarily goes to the part of his body that is being touched. This buys you time to come forward with offense. You must also be cautious of your own tendency to freeze. Again, use the first touch concept as your window of opportunity.

**Momentum And First Touch, Chapter 3.**

## INDUCING THE ATTACK

If you know in advance when your opponent is going to attack, you are at a great advantage. An armed attacker, especially, is likely to be tense and nervous, and will respond to any unpredictable move you make. You may be able to induce the attack by giving your opponent a perceived opportunity to commit.

**Recognizing The Attack, Chapter 12.**

## INERTIA

Inertia is resistance to change in motion. A heavy person has more inertia than a lightweight, and a person moving at a great speed has more inertia than a person moving at a slower speed. This makes the heavy or fast fighter difficult to stop. However, inertia also applies to starting motion. Thus, a heavy fighter has more inertia to overcome when setting himself in motion than a lightweight. This bit of knowledge can work to your advantage when executing a takedown. If your opponent is heavy, once he hits the ground, he has to expend a considerable amount of energy getting back to his feet, which may afford you an opportunity to escape.

**Scenario 6, Chapter 13.**

## INHERENT WEAKNESS

Many targets that win a fight in sports martial arts are not effective within the short time frame of a street encounter. Since there are no rules or bell to signal the end of the round, you must focus on taking your opponent out as quickly as possible. Try to attack targets on your opponent's body that are inherently weak. Knees, groin, throat, and eyes are examples of such targets. If you decide to further subdue him on the ground, a choke or joint break may be a good option. When practicing how to attack the inherent weakness, take into consideration the confines of the area, and identify finishing techniques that would eliminate the threat in the least number of moves.

**Target Areas For Softening Techniques, Chapter 2.**

**Attacking an inherently weak target can end a fight instantly. Be aware of the potentially lethal consequences of a strike to the throat.**

## MIND AND BODY FOCUS

Your opponent can be defeated easier if you separate his mind and body focus. Try interrupting your opponent's concentration through a distraction. This can be a non-contact move, such as a sudden twitch of your body, or it can be a softening strike. When your opponent's focus is broken, you have created a window of opportunity for your unbalancing move. By the same token, you must strive to keep your own mind and body focus intact.

**Three Points Of Pain, Chapter 11.**

**If your attempt to unbalance your opponent fails, shift your focus to a different target. For example, let go of his neck and attack his leg.**

## MISALIGNING THE BODY'S POSTURE

Any time your opponent's body is not in its "natural state," he loses strength, and unbalancing him is easier. Misaligning the body's posture is therefore a prerequisite for a takedown. For example, twisting your opponent's upper body, while keeping his foundation from moving, misaligns his posture. You can also think of this in terms of immobilizing one part of your opponent's body, while keeping another part moving. If your opponent's lower body isn't allowed to move comfortably with his upper body, his center of gravity will fall outside of his foundation, and he will lose balance. The push-pull principle, along with many natural barriers in the environment, can be used to misalign your opponent's posture and cause a loss of balance.

**The Inherent Weaknesses Of Your Stance, Chapter 1.**

## MOMENTUM

Momentum is a combination of mass (weight) and velocity (speed). Even if you are lightweight, a considerable amount of momentum can help you move through a barrier or knock your opponent off balance. It is our natural reaction to want to stop or slow down when confronted with a barrier or threat. However, if you allow a break in momentum, you cannot benefit fully from your weight. When engaging your opponent is inevitable, you must do so with full determination to carry the momentum of your techniques through to the finish. Any halt or break in momentum will negate your power and give your opponent a window of opportunity to defeat you. Once you have engaged your adversary for a takedown or throw, make an effort to increase his momentum. The faster he moves, the more chaotic the takedown or throw is, and the more difficult it is for him to counter your attack.

**Momentum And The Push Pull Principle, Chapter 3.**

## MOVING OFF THE ATTACK LINE

When a strike or weapon is about to be used against you, your first concern should be to thwart the attack by moving off the attack line. When up against a knife wielding opponent, consider how he is holding the weapon. Try to place yourself in the superior position slightly toward your opponent's back. Keep your escape routes in mind, and do not move into a position where you might get trapped. Think about how to follow up with an unbalancing move once you have allowed your opponent's attack to miss.

**Recognizing The Attack, Chapter 12.**

## NO SENSITIVITY PRINCIPLE

Weapons lack sensitivity; you are unable to feel, through the weapon, how much damage you are doing to your opponent. This is true whether you use the weapon for striking or pressing. Be aware that it is easy to do a lot of damage fast when armed with any kind of weapon. However, don't be afraid to use it when your safety is at stake.

**Weapon Presses, Chapter 7.**

## OFFENSIVE DEFENSE

Effective self-defense includes an element of offense. Taking the offensive approach means taking the active approach. Rather than responding to events as they unfold before you, interfere with them before they have unfolded. In a takedown situation, this might mean closing distance and initiating the takedown, through the use of momentum and the element of surprise, the moment you recognize that there is a sufficient threat to your safety.

**Offense vs. Defense, Chapter 12.**

**Your opponent's momentum can work either for or against you. If he tackles you, his momentum may place you on the ground with him (above). If you side-step the tackle and allow his momentum to continue, it may unbalance him, while you are still standing (below).**

## OVER AND UNDER PRINCIPLE

This principle is similar in concept to the push-pull principle, and is used to misalign your opponent's posture in preparation for an unbalancing move. For example, face your opponent and wrap your right arm over the top of his left arm, and your left arm underneath his right arm. This creates leverage and the ability to use opposing movements to tilt or twist your opponent's body out of alignment with his center of gravity.

**Misaligning The Posture On The Ground, Chapter 13.**

## PERCEPTION OF THREAT

How you perceive the situation may determine your response to a threat. For example, if a weapon is involved, you may be much more cautious moving in for the takedown than you would if the opponent were empty handed. Although the principle used for unbalancing an adversary is the same regardless of whether there is a weapon involved or not, how you respond may work either to your advantage or disadvantage. It is therefore important to train for all possible scenarios and threat levels. To avoid getting "blinded" by your opponent's weapon, try to treat it as an extension of his arm.

**Using The Knife Offensively, Chapter 12.**

## POSITION OF SUPERIORITY

The ability to move yourself to a superior position minimizes your opponent's strength and places him in a position of vulnerability. The superior position is normally behind your opponent. You can attain the superior position by maneuvering yourself toward your opponent's back, or by maneuvering your opponent with his back toward you, as in a circular takedown using neck manipulation. Attaining the superior position also buys you time, as your opponent can't execute an effective attack against you until he has repositioned himself along the attack line.

**Positioning Preparatory To The Takedown, Chapter 2.**

A verbal confrontation escalates, and your opponent grabs your shirt, and prepares to punch you with his other hand.

Can you side-step and use outside superiority to unbalance him forward?

## POUNDS PER SQUARE INCH

This concept works great for presses. The smaller the surface area, and the harder the weapon you use in the press, the greater the pounds per square inch. Pressing with your elbow, for example, enables you to use considerable pounds per square inch. Because the elbow is small, hard, and pointed, it will dig deeply into the target. For maximum effect, place your full body weight directly above the press.

**Weapon Presses, Chapter 7.**

## PUSH-PULL PRINCIPLE

Both sides of your body should share the workload equally. You accomplish this by immobilizing the target and using opposing forces around a rotational axis. Pushing against one of your opponent's shoulders, while pulling on the other, creates a rotation in his upper body that misaligns his posture and causes a loss of balance. Another example of the push-pull principle is when a joint lock is involved. For example, in a leg takedown, pull your opponent's heel toward you, while pushing against his thigh right above his knee. The joint (knee) is isolated and controlled by going against the joint's natural range of motion. The same principle applies to the elbow. Note that the principle of two points of balance is related to the push-pull principle. In order to unbalance an adversary, attain two points of balance and start a rotation around an axis mid-way between them. The farther apart these points are, the more leverage you attain, and the easier the takedown is. However, be careful with placing yourself in a position where you have to overextend your center of gravity by reaching.

**The Push-Pull Principle, Chapter 3.**

## RESETTING THE BODY'S BALANCE

Any time you make a move, your body must be given the opportunity to correct itself. If you extend your arm, you will eventually withdraw it again. If you kick, you will eventually replant that foot on the ground. And if you duck a punch, your body will eventually come back up again. Knowledge of this concept helps you time your attack to your opponent's weakest moment. If you can make his first strike, kick, or grab attempt miss, you have a brief window of opportunity for your unbalancing move, while his body corrects itself.

**Defining Balance, Chapter 1.**

## ROTATIONAL INERTIA

In a technique that involves circular motion, the farther the mass is from the center of rotation, the more difficult it is to move the mass. In a circular takedown, keeping your opponent as close to your own center of mass as possible saves you energy and speeds up the unbalancing technique.
**Reverse Throw From Figure Four Lock (points to consider), Chapter 9.**

## SAFETY IN CLOSENESS

Avoiding an attack should always be a priority. However, an unbalancing move cannot be executed unless you are close enough to make contact with your opponent. Furthermore, many techniques that are designed for medium or long range fighting lose much of their power if thrown from close range. The roundhouse kick is one such technique. If you can move to close range and inside of the kick's path of power, you also create for yourself a window of opportunity to unbalance your adversary, while he is still in the process of kicking.
**Reverse Throw From Double Hand Neck Manipulation, Chapter 9.**

**When it is not possible to remove yourself from the situation, an unbalancing move requiring closeness may be a good option.**

## SENSORY OVERLOAD

If you split your opponent's mind and body focus through a multitude of strikes to different targets, you have created sensory overload. Once your opponent's focus is split, you have a better chance to engage him for the takedown. A multitude of strikes in rapid succession can also make your opponent backpedal. This automatically places him in a disadvantaged position. You can now use your momentum, along with your opponent's split focus, to successfully take him down.

**Target Exercise, Chapter 2.**

## THREE PHASES OF CONTROLLING

A takedown rarely works if we try to match strength with strength. It is therefore important to separate your opponent's mind and body focus before attempting the takedown. The first phase of controlling your adversary is the softening and distraction phase, where you break your opponent's concentration on his attack. The second phase is the controlling phase, or the takedown itself, where you execute the actual unbalancing move. The third phase is the finish, where you eliminate the threat by fleeing to safety, or by further subduing your opponent on the ground.

**The Stages Of A Threat, Chapter 11.**

## THREE ZONES OF FIGHTING

The Safety Zone is where you and your opponent are unable to reach each other with any type of technique. The Safety Zone for an empty handed encounter differs from a weapon encounter. The Out-Fighting Zone is where you and your opponent can reach each other with long range techniques only. Most punching and kicking occur in the Out-Fighting Zone. The In-Fighting Zone is where you and your opponent are touching, or within a few inches of each other. This is the distance used for most takedowns, throws, and presses. In the In-Fighting Zone, look for ways to trap your opponent's limbs or to manipulate his balance. Moving from the In-Fighting or Out-Fighting Zone to the Safety Zone may be difficult when up against an aggressive opponent. The ability to judge the distance to your opponent helps you take advantage of the three zones of fighting.

**Your Zone Of Safety, Chapter 2.**

## TIMING

In order to successfully unbalance your opponent, you must know when to close distance and when to wait. Good timing allows you to take advantage of your window of opportunity. Sometimes timing means initiating an action instead of waiting to respond to one. Drawing an action from your opponent through a sudden, unexpected move can help you with proper timing of your counter-attack. Timing also involves moving in at the appropriate moment and smothering your opponent's technique.

**Timing, Chapter 2.**

## TORQUE

Torque is the lever arm times the force. You can create a mechanical strength advantage by utilizing a lever arm that is as long as possible. For example, if catching your opponent's leg in the crook of your arm with the intent to throw him off balance to the rear, less strength is needed if you catch his leg as close to his foot as possible, rather than close to his knee or hip.

**Lever Arm, Chapter 3.**

## TWO POINTS OF BALANCE

For a takedown to be effective, you must manipulate two points of balance simultaneously, one high and one low. When attacking two widely separated points, use both your hands and feet to avoid reaching or overextending your center of gravity. For example, tilt your opponent's head back with a palm press, and simultaneously immobilize his foundation by placing your leg behind his.

**The Push-Pull Principle, Chapter 3.**

## WINDOW OF OPPORTUNITY

This is the moment you can successfully engage your opponent for the takedown or throw. If you lose your window of opportunity, you must create a new one, or it will be a matter of your strength against your opponent's. Sometimes a window of opportunity is very brief, but if you create it with full knowledge and intent (through a distraction followed by an unbalancing move, for example), you can still act on it successfully. Other concepts, like first touch, can also be used to create a window of opportunity.

**Your Window Of Opportunity, Chapter 1.**

# 1  Overview of Takedowns

The purpose of a takedown is to get your opponent on the ground without going down with him. Because loss of balance is such a chaotic feeling, taking your adversary down gives you additional time to execute a finishing technique or escape to safety. Most fights can be broken down into the following stages:

1. The stand-up fight
2. The takedown
3. The ground fight

Many fighters, depending on their purpose and goal, limit their skills to one of these stages. Most karate practitioners and sport kickboxers fight within the perimeters of the first stage. A judo practitioner fights mostly within the perimeters of the second stage. And a jiu-jitsu practitioner fights mainly within the perimeters of the last stage. In the free-style or no-holds-barred events the practitioners are more often seen using all three stages, going from stand-up to takedown to ground fight. The style you practice and the type of competitions you take part in will determine which fighting stage should be the focus of your training. However, the takedown phase has a clear advantage: once your opponent hits the ground, for the next few seconds you are the sole person to determine whether to continue the fight or escape to safety. Mastering the takedown phase is therefore important for those learning the arts for self-defense rather than for sports.

## Lesson Objectives

At the end of this lesson, you should understand:

1. How stability is determined
2. How stance affects stability
3. How to estimate the location of the center of gravity
4. The physical and mental elements of shifting the center of gravity
5. How to counteract your opponent's tendency to retain stability
6. How to counteract your opponent's tendency to unbalance you

We will now define the primary principle of physics used in a takedown, and then look at the physical and mental elements involved.

# Defining Balance

The primary principle of physics used in a takedown is the position of the *center of gravity*. In layman's terms, this can be thought of as the balance point. In order for any person or object to retain balance, the center of gravity must be above the area of the foundation of that person or object. If you can disturb your opponent's center of gravity so that it no longer falls above the area of his foundation, he will lose balance regardless of how big, strong, aggressive, or smart he is.

### *Center of gravity = balance point*

When you have good physical balance, you can utilize your techniques to their maximum potential. When you are off balance, you are unable to use your strength and techniques effectively. When you become part of a physical confrontation, it is to your benefit to retain your own balance while striving to unbalance your opponent. Once you have unbalanced your opponent, you should ideally keep him off balance until you are able to subdue him or flee to safety. In all of the exercises and scenarios we will explore in this book, the center of gravity is the one principle that you must always keep in mind. Once you learn how to manipulate your opponent's center of gravity, the takedown is not only possible, it is *certain*, regardless of your own or your opponent's physical characteristics. The center of gravity will hereafter be referred to as the C.G.

**The closer the C.G. is to the limits of its "envelope," the easier it is to lose balance. The envelope can be thought of as the width and depth of your stance.**

**Because the stability envelope is small, the C.G. only needs to shift a short distance to create a loss of balance.**

Upright stance, high center of gravity = less stable. The narrow stance is, in itself, not unstable, but losing balance is easier because of the rigidity of the body and the high C.G.

**You do not need to keep your upper body rigid. Leaning forward, back, or to the side is possible without losing balance, as long as the center of gravity falls above the foundation.**

The center of gravity is normally located near the center of your upper body. However, your physical build or stance can affect the exact location of the center of gravity. When you are standing upright, your center of gravity is higher than when you are in a crouched stance. The lower the center of gravity, the more stable you are. It can therefore be said that if you want to retain balance, you should lower your center of gravity, and if you want to unbalance your opponent, you should attack when his center of gravity is high. However, this advice is not always easy to implement. In a street confrontation, you don't necessarily know when somebody might attack you, which might preclude you from lowering your center of gravity at the right moment. Likewise, you might not have the time or opportunity to attack when your opponent's center of gravity is high. We must therefore look at ways to raise our opponent's center of gravity during the course of the confrontation, or more importantly, to place it outside of the area of his foundation.

**A wide stance is more stable than a narrow stance, because it covers a larger surface area.**

Crouched stance, low center of gravity = more stable. In addition to being more stable, the crouched stance also creates a threatening impression, giving you a mental advantage.

**Although a wide stance is very stable, there are some drawbacks. It is difficult to cover ground quickly from a wide stance. When in the danger zone, and it is apparent that you have to fight, widen your base, preferably with one foot forward and one foot back.**

When somebody approaches you in a threatening manner or reaches out to strike or grab you, your natural reaction is to shy away. This is done through a flinch or through movement of your upper body to the rear, which usually results in the head and center of gravity moving to a high position and close to the limits of its envelope. This reaction is intended to help you avoid an attack, but it does not take into consideration what happens after the initial threat. If your opponent advances and throws a strike, and you flinch to the rear, you are in a bad position to counter. Because your upper body and weight have moved to the rear, there is a conflict with the direction of energy, which precludes you from establishing momentum through the use of your body weight. Although this is a natural reaction, and not much can be done about it if you are taken by surprise, as soon as you have established the fact that there is a threat, lower your center of gravity slightly and protect your head by keeping your chin tucked down toward your chest.

Note that momentum is established through a combination of motion and weight. Since nobody is weightless, and there is not much you can do about your weight at any given moment, the determining factor becomes motion. The motion must act in the direction of your intended attack in order to benefit you. In regards to linear momentum, you must move toward your opponent in order to use your momentum against him.

**Try this:** When is it easiest to take a quick step forward? When your body is rigid, upright, or leaning slightly to the rear? Or when your body is relaxed, "heavy," and slightly crouched?

You can fool your mind to ready itself for an advance by keeping your center of gravity slightly low and prepared to move forward to create momentum. Face a partner and have him throw a quick strike in your direction (close enough to make you feel a need to react, but far enough that it doesn't actually land). React with the natural movement of bringing your head and upper body to the rear. Immediately attempt to take a quick step forward. This is difficult because your mind is thinking "get away," so you must first convince it to move forward. Do the same exercise again, but force yourself to take a quick step forward, and to a slight angle to the side avoiding the strike, at the initiation of your partner's attack. Can you feel how it is easier to move in for the takedown when you establish an aggressive mind-set from the start? Utilizing your momentum this way also places you ahead of your opponent mentally. He does not expect you to take charge of the situation and execute an unbalancing move against him. It also saves you time, because your move is already under way the moment he initiates the attack.

**Think about this**

**If you shy away, you have to reset your body's balance forward before being able to utilize your momentum.**

Note that I'm not saying that moving to the rear to avoid a strike is wrong; only that you should be aware of what it takes to reset your body's balance.

## The Inherent Weaknesses of Your Stance

The way one normally walks is not ideal for stability. Instability is caused when you cross your legs to take a step. Your stance is now narrow, or worse, you are on one foot. When your opponent tries to unbalance you, ideally he is looking for when you raise one foot to step. When you get within distance for an unbalancing technique to occur, keep both feet firmly planted and slightly apart, with your knees bent. Note that mobility is an important element in any confrontation, and a stance that is too wide or low tends to counter your ability to move or reposition yourself.

The wider your base, and the lower your center of gravity, the more stable you are. But this does not mean that you always want to maintain a low and wide stance, as such a stance may hinder your mobility. The best stance is the one that feels comfortable and comes naturally, so there must be some leeway when selecting your stance. Also consider your flexibility. If you are stiff, you are much easier to unbalance than if you have flexibility to move with the forces. Flexibility allows you to adjust for shifts in C.G., to move faster, get off the ground quicker, and endure pressure against joints better. This is one reason why you should stay flexible into old age. Being flexible is not necessarily equivalent to doing full splits or kicking to the head, as there are many low targets that are effective when attacked properly. Think of flexibility as a defense quality. Being flexible helps you guard against injuries in self-defense and every day life.

Analyze where your opponent's stance is naturally weak and how to take advantage of it. Next, analyze how to "break" the stability of a strong stance by misaligning your opponent's body. For example, if he is in a wide horse stance, misalign his stability by twisting his upper body to a perpendicular angle, or by bending it forward or to the rear. If your opponent is in a toe-to-heel stance, misalign his stability by sweeping one of his feet toward his centerline.

**Reminder** **Whenever your opponent's upper body is not properly aligned with his lower body, you can unbalance him easier.**

Use your hands, feet, or body to push or twist your partner's body. Later on, when you have learned more about takedowns, take time to practice them in tight places, like a hallway or small bathroom. If you can't move your body to start significant momentum, can you still unbalance your opponent? If there is a barrier behind you, like a wall that your opponent has slammed you against, can you still unbalance him? What if your opponent is the one against the wall? How can you unbalance him if you can't move his upper body to the rear? Experiment with breaking your partner's postural alignment when you only have one direction (example: along the hallway) in which to move.

## Balance Exercise

Maintain balance when pushed by widening your base, taking a step, or adjusting your body to compensate for the shift in C.G. For example, if kicked in the midsection, move your hips to the rear and your upper body forward. If kicked to chest, it is more difficult to remain stable by moving the body alone, and a step is generally required. Knowing this in advance helps you attack targets on your opponent's body that are likely to disturb his balance.

1. How easy or difficult is it to regain stability when pushed off balance? Have a partner push you, lightly at first, from a variety of angles. Note how long it takes for you to regain your composure. This gives you an idea of your time frame when executing an unbalancing technique on your opponent, especially if it doesn't result in a full takedown.

2. Have your partner approach you from behind and push lightly against your upper back. Note your natural tendency to take a step forward with one foot to brace yourself.

3. Next have your partner approach you from the front and push you hard enough to make you take a step back with one foot to brace yourself. Which comes more natural, stepping forward or stepping back? Most people would say that stepping forward is easier. We can therefore establish that it is easier to unbalance an opponent to the rear. However, this is not the same as saying that a frontal attack is better than a rear attack.

4. The best time to try an unbalancing move is when your opponent's foundation is narrow; for example, when he is in the process of stepping. Have your partner walk naturally at a slow pace. Approach him from the side, and push against his shoulder. Time the push to when he has just raised one foot to take a step. Push hard enough to get him to stumble.

## Shifting the Center of Gravity

The primary reason you would take an adversary down is to keep him from fighting back. This gives you time to get to safety. There are many ways one can shift an adversary's center of gravity to effect a takedown. For example:

**Reminder**   **Push the upper body back until the center of gravity no longer falls above the foundation.**

**Stable.**

**Not as stable.**

**Loss of balance.**

___

**Your push must be determined and done with intent. Do not let up until you feel your opponent going down.**

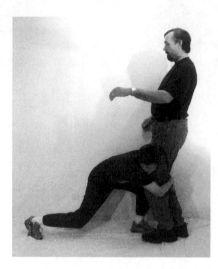

Shifting the foundation away from the center of gravity is a little more difficult, because it requires you to duck low. You are also working against your opponent's greater body mass.

A simultaneous push against his upper body makes it easier to unbalance him. Pull his leg toward you and drive forward with your shoulder against his thigh.

If you allow your opponent to take a step back to brace himself, he will widen his base and retain balance. You should therefore strive to immobilize both of his legs.

The circular move has the potential to create a lot or momentum. This causes a chaotic feeling, which splits your opponent's mind and body focus. It is therefore a good strategic move, but not always possible in a self-defense situation.

Pull your opponent in a circle, until his feet are "lagging behind" his upper body center of gravity.

All of the above applies to a person who is standing. But it is equally possible to shift the center of gravity of a person on the ground. The same principle applies: if the center of gravity is not above the area of the foundation, he will lose balance. No exceptions! It is often enough to shift only part of your opponent's foundation in order to create a loss of balance. For example, if your opponent is on all four, shifting the position of one of his hands may be enough to unbalance him.

Pulling up on your opponent's arm, while pushing down on his shoulder, makes it easier to unbalance him.

If your opponent is on all four, shift his balance by pulling one hand out from under him.

**Moving your opponent's hand to a wider "stance" allows the C.G. to stay above the foundation. He will therefore retain balance.**

**Moving your opponent's hand to a narrower "stance" by kicking it, for example, makes the C.G. fall outside of the foundation, and he will drop, face first, to the ground.**

It is easier to take your opponent's balance rearward than forward, because his body does not naturally bend to the rear very far. A kick, strike, or push to a natural bend in his body (back of knee, small of back, etc.) will bring his upper body to the rear, aiding you with the takedown.

**A kick to the back of the knee assumes that you have the superior position from the start, which also gives you the option to run rather than fight. However, this move can be used as a rescue technique when coming to the aid of another person.**

A kick to a natural bend in the body, such as the back of the knee, helps you unbalance your opponent to the rear.

The kick to the back of the knee will be more effective if you can also attack a second target on your opponent's upper body – a sharp pull on the shoulder, for example.

**You must pull back continually, never allowing your opponent to regain balance, until the takedown is certain.**

**Pulling your opponent forward is not as effective. Since his body moves naturally this way, it is easier for him to retain balance. If trying this unbalancing move, it must be done forcefully to keep your opponent from compensating for the shift in C.G.**

Note that your body should be slightly crouched for balance and momentum.

Whether grabbing your opponent from the front or rear, when pulling him toward you and stepping back, your power is along your centerline. When using a straight unbalancing technique, bring your elbows toward the center of your body. If your elbows are sticking out to the sides, it is difficult focusing your power. Test the centerline concept in everyday life when lifting. You will seem to have more strength when lifting heavy objects, if you hold them close to the centerline of your body.

Once your opponent goes down, the first thing on his mind is to get back up again. If the situation warrants a continuation, the best time to attack with a new unbalancing move is when he is just beginning to get back up. An opponent on the ground is most stable when he is either flat on his back or flat on his stomach. The next most stable state is on all four. The natural progression is for him to raise one hand and start to push himself up. This is the time to attack: when his foundation is just *beginning* to become unstable.

## Line of Power Exercise

Your greatest stability is along the greatest width of your stance. Stability is also determined by the proximity of the applied force to your center of gravity, and by how flexible you are to bend with the forces.

1. Have your partner stand with his feet side by side. Push his upper body straight back, but don't allow him to take a step. Note how quickly he loses balance. This is because the strength of his stance is not along the line of power.

2. Have your partner stand with one foot forward and one foot back. Push his upper body back until he loses balance. As you can see, this takes quite a bit of effort. We can therefore say that if we can keep our opponent's foundation from moving, we can unbalance him easier.

3. When kicking your adversary, a straight kick like the front kick is best, because the power is straight ahead. Practice the front kick with extension in the hips. By extending the hips forward and simultaneously straightening the knee, you will create a powerful *thrust* with your full weight behind the kick.

## The Elements of Takedowns

Keep the following elements in mind throughout your study:

1. **Shifting your opponent's center of gravity.** In general, the easiest way to do this is by moving his upper body to the rear. An added benefit is that this also limits the use of his eyesight and the use of his hands.

2. **The use of momentum.** Momentum is a combination of your weight and your speed, and can be applied either in a straight line or in a circle. In general, takedowns tend to be more chaotic if you use circular momentum.

*Momentum = mass (weight) X velocity (speed)*

Circular motion combined with balance manipulation enables you to take down a bigger and stronger opponent without having to out-muscle him. This is true regardless of whether you use a joint lock, a leg takedown, or other balance manipulation.

3. **The element of surprise.** Superior positioning and swiftness in the execution of your technique limits your opponent's ability to respond. Don't hesitate. Once you start with the takedown, there is no stopping.

4. **The sense of touch.** Your sense of touch may be even more vital than your eyesight. Once you learn to "feel" your opponent's balance point, you can succeed with the takedown even if you are blindfolded.

## Your Window of Opportunity

We often talk about self-*defense*, yet the offensive move offers a better understanding of the workings of the human body and mind, which, in turn, translates into ability to predict and negate a takedown. The most common action when we start going down is trying to regain our balance. If I were to give you a forceful push, what would be your natural reaction without even thinking about it? You would take a step back and brace yourself. If you allow your opponent's foundation (his feet) to keep up with the center of gravity of his upper body, the takedown will fail. This is true whether you push your opponent back or pull him in a circle. To counteract this, you must shift your opponent's center of gravity so quickly that his slower reaction time keeps him from stepping with the technique, or you must present some sort of barrier that physically prevents him from stepping (by tripping him simultaneous to your upper body attack, for example).

**Keeping your opponent's foundation stationary with your own leg, while shifting his center of gravity to the rear, increases the effectiveness of the takedown.**

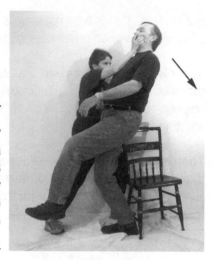

**Tripping your opponent over a barrier keeps his foundation stationary and increases the effectiveness of the takedown.**

**It is not always possible to keep your opponent from moving his foundation, especially if he has lifted you off the ground.**

As already discussed, our natural reaction when attacked is to try to avoid the attack by flinching to the rear. This has several disadvantages. First, you are raising your center of gravity, making you less stable. Second, it is difficult to backpedal quickly, especially when your upper body is leaning to the rear. This makes you less mobile. Third, if your goal is to close distance for a takedown, your body must first reset to the forward crouch before you can advance and use your momentum against your opponent. Fourth, flinching or leaning back keeps you from using the concept of *first touch*, which allows you to take advantage of your window of opportunity while your opponent is still absorbed in his attack.

**Reminder**

**Your window of opportunity is when your opponent is momentarily distracted, either by something you say, or do, or by something he says or does.**

It is difficult not to react defensively when attacked, especially if you have no prior experience with fighting. You must therefore start by practicing with a partner you trust. Have him wear boxing gloves and attack you, stepping forward with each strike and using light contact only. Instead of trying to get away, your mind-set should be to block or parry and intercept, while simultaneously moving forward to close distance for a takedown. This requires that you keep your weight in a crouched stance. Often, safety is in distance, but sometimes, as when you can't get away, or when you want to use a takedown, safety is in closeness. If you can get to the inside of your opponent's attack, you are safer than if you stay at his optimal striking or grabbing range.

Most people find it difficult to throw an effective strike or kick from very close range, and once you come forward, your opponent will have a natural tendency to move back to where he is again comfortable. Your focus is not on trying to get away, but on trying to counter with an unbalancing move. This involves getting past his offense. Once this mind-set is established, you will start to turn the situation to your advantage, where you become the aggressor. I'm not suggesting that you should allow an assailant to grab you, but it is important to understand how your window of opportunity works. Be aware and evaluate the situation beforehand, identifying your avenues of escape. Attacks seldom start with a surprise punch. There is usually something leading up to the physical attack: for example, a verbal argument. If there is a chance to get away or de-escalate the situation before it becomes physical, this should always be your priority.

The one thing that should be learned about takedowns is that they all work off of the same principles, with slight variations in technique. If you can learn the principles rather than one technique for each of the many hundred variations that can occur, your overall ability to adapt and defend yourself will improve considerably. Throughout the course of your study, we will examine ways to strengthen these principles by combining several different laws of physics. We will also work from a variety of positions and experiment with many different techniques, including trapping of legs, arms, and neck. However, we will always keep in mind, and refer back to, the primary principle of balance: the location of the center of gravity.

**Reminder**

**There is a difference between knowing how a technique works and being able to execute it. There is a difference between executing a technique against a willing partner, and executing it against an unwilling opponent intent on hurting you.**

# What Can Go Wrong?

Avoid situations that can lead to potential problems. This may seem like an impossible concept to follow that would eventually lead to paranoia, but I'm of a different opinion. You don't *have* to hang out at bars late at night, you don't *have* to walk alone to your car at night, there *are* measures you can take to keep your home secure, it *is* possible to roll up your car windows and lock the doors when stopped at an intersection at night or in a secluded area. Use common sense, be honest and stand by your principles, don't behave inappropriately, don't be rude to others, don't hitchhike or pick up hitchhikers, don't go with a stranger in his car when your own has broken down, etc. Make the decision beforehand that when you're at a party or social gathering, if hostility toward any person manifests itself, it is time to leave, even if it isn't directed toward you initially. Decide beforehand exactly how far you will go if confronted by a stranger. For example, if you have made the decision that under no circumstances will you go with him in his car, it is easier to stand by that decision later and defend against the attack all out, should you need to. If you have thought about it beforehand, you are less likely to freeze or try to talk your way out of a helpless and dangerous situation, and more likely to take charge with an appropriate defense.

# Common Mistakes

### 1. Not understanding the body's balance.

Your opponent can be unbalanced through head or upper body manipulation, by removing his foundation, through straight or circular momentum, or through a combination of these. Regardless of which technique you use, your focus must be toward the ground. Two points of balance, one high and one low, should be manipulated simultaneously.

### 2. Failing to keep your own center of gravity low and above your foundation.

An upright or tense posture makes it easier for your opponent to unbalance you.

### 3. Believing that a technique is foolproof.

You can learn all you can get your hands on, yet there is always that element of unpredictability. However, if you understand the scientific principles of the center of gravity in balance and takedowns, you also know what to look for in your opponent's tries to counter your move.

# 2 Positioning and Timing

The biggest challenge about taking somebody down is not the takedown itself, but getting into position to execute the takedown. In order to achieve an advantage, your position must be superior to your opponent's. Many techniques are initially equally superior. If your opponent has the size or strength advantage, the best you can do is try to improve your position.

**Two people squaring off for battle are initially in equally superior positions. The stronger person is likely to win.**

**An object in the environment, such as a wall or a chair, can improve the position of the weaker fighter. The object hinders your opponent's mobility, especially if placed behind him, where you can also use it to destroy his balance.**

**The ability to use leverage can improve the odds for the weaker person.**

**Leverage against the elbow can be used to turn your opponent to the inferior position with his back toward you.**

The superior position is generally behind your opponent's back, for the following reasons:

1. You can rely on the element of surprise.
2. You can limit the use of your opponent's eyesight, hands, and feet.
3. The human body does not naturally bend to the rear, so it is easier to take your adversary down.

However, there are many other positions that are superior and lend themselves to takedowns. In addition, you will not always be able to decide how to position in relation to your opponent. A threatening situation, especially if you are taken by surprise, ends up the way it ends up. You must therefore know how to shift your opponent's C.G. from any position.

# Lesson Objectives

At the end of this lesson, you should understand:

1. The stages of a takedown
2. How to determine the superior position
3. How to split your opponent's focus and use a set-up for closing distance
4. How speed is crucial, and why broken momentum will make the takedown fail
5. How your adversary's joints (neck, elbows, knees) can aid you with the takedown
6. Why timing and softening techniques are crucial
7. When safety is in closeness
8. How to establish your zone of safety

# The Stages of a Takedown

There are several parts of the takedown that must be practiced:

- First, the scenario that sets it up. This includes the environment and the situation that brings about a threat.

- Second, the entry into the self-defense technique. Should you initiate or wait until your opponent initiates? When does it become clear that you will have to defend yourself? When do you know that you no longer have the opportunity to walk away?

- Third, the actual physical engagement of the technique. Do you wait until your opponent touches or locks onto you, or do you take the first step and throw a strike to distract or hurt him?

- Fourth, the actual takedown. What environmental factors must you be aware of? Are there barriers or dead ends? Is your footing slippery or solid? How do you continue if you lose balance? How do you continue if the opponent resists or if the takedown fails?

- Fifth, the stage after the takedown. Your window of opportunity to escape is the moment your opponent hits the ground. Again, take into consideration the environment and your ability to escape. Are you hurt? Can you run? If a friend is involved, might it be better to subdue your opponent on the ground, while your friend calls for help?

- Sixth, what to do after it's over. When do you report to authorities and when don't you? Or is it always necessary to report?

All of the above, except for the last one, might be a matter of a split second decision. But the severity of the threat will always dictate your decision. How hurt are you or the opponent? Is there a weapon involved? If it is a knife or firearm, can you find it and take custody of it, so that it won't be used against you during your escape? There are no definite answers to these questions. Much of what you do depends on your physical condition and mental composure, and on how much prior thought you have given the situation.

## Positioning Preparatory to the Takedown

If you are in an imminent fistfight, the superior position is slightly toward your opponent's back, because this limits the use of most of his weapons. If he stands with his right side forward, the superior position is toward his right side. However, there are other factors that must be considered when selecting a position. For example, what are the escape routes? If you move behind your opponent, are you simultaneously trapping yourself in a corner or against a wall? Sometimes the situation warrants a compromise on positioning. You must also take your opponent's mobility into consideration. Does he attack in a straight line? Assuming that you can't escape, try to move slightly toward his weak side (his back). Does he try to circle you into a corner or against a wall? Prevent it by stepping the opposite direction he is circling. This will close the distance between you, so you must be ready to engage in the takedown.

**Your Mindset** **Be aware of your positioning and take the active approach to improve it.**

## Positioning Exercise

It is difficult to execute a technique when your body isn't properly aligned with the attack line. For example, throw a strike with your right hand at somebody who is standing by your left shoulder. The technique requires that you move to change the angle to your opponent. This takes time, giving your opponent the opportunity to beat you to the punch, flee, or take you down. Your position is therefore inferior. The superior position, on the other hand, buys *you* time when you need it.

1. Face a partner from a distance of approximately ten feet. Regardless of the direction your partner moves, try to position so that you are always at a slight off-angle toward his back. If he switches stance, the superior position will change.

2. Face a partner from a distance of approximately twenty feet. Have him rush toward you as fast as he can without warning. How easy or difficult is it to side-step the attack? Do the same exercise from a distance of ten feet. The speed with which distance closes is seldom taken into consideration when training for escapes.

## Positioning During the Takedown

A takedown requires physical control, or some form of grab. For example:

1. You are grabbed by surprise.
2. You initiate the grab by seizing an opportunity.

When grabbed, whether by surprise or otherwise, we have a natural tendency to fight the arm that grabs us. This is true regardless of the type of grab. If your opponent places his hands around your neck, your hands will automatically come up and grab his in an attempt to make him let go. If he grabs you around the waist, your hands will again end up on his. The problem is that you are fighting your opponent at his point of strength. If an adversary grabs you, his concerted effort and focus is in that grab. So if you are smaller or weaker than him, you are using your lesser strength against his greater strength, which is strategically unsound, and your attempt to escape will most likely fail. Avoiding fighting your opponent at the grip requires some training to reprogram your mind-set. Because your opponent's focus is on the grip, he will be inattentive to his balance point, allowing you to act with an unbalancing technique.

**Your Mindset**

**Don't fight your opponent at the grip.
Go for an unbalancing technique instead.**

Positioning during this phase of the fight is equally important. If possible, place your opponent in a naturally weak position, either by initiating the move or by making your opponent move. Sometimes it is easier, and usually more economical, to make your opponent move, especially if you can gain control of his head.

If it is not a surprise attack, and you have determined that escape is not possible, you might be better off initiating the takedown by seizing an opportunity. For example, if your opponent reaches out to grab you, his focus will be on the grab. This is your window of opportunity to explode forward with an unbalancing move. An explosive advance places you to the inside of his technique. As long as you follow-up, this is an example of where safety is in closeness rather than in distance. If possible, step slightly toward your opponent's weak side rather than straight toward the attack line.

**If you end up along the attack line (your opponent's centerline), drive a knee into his groin simultaneous with your advance.**

Initiate your gap closure and unbalancing move when your opponent reaches out to grab you.

Be careful not to step into your opponent's strike. Sometimes a slight delay, or a parry or block, can work to your advantage. Blocks or parries can freeze your opponent for a split second, making your advance possible.

# How to Approach the Opponent's Joints

Pay attention to the positioning of your opponent's larger joints: neck, elbows, and knees. Because the joints only bend in one direction, working against the natural movement of the joints allows you to manipulate your opponent's balance easier. When he can't bend his joints, he has to go in the direction you are taking him, or risk serious injury.

The arms bend forward, so when attacking the arms, try to position behind or to the side of the elbow. The legs bend backward, so if using a leg takedown, position in front of or slightly to the side of your opponent. The neck bends in all directions. However, the body bends forward easier than to the rear, and since the neck is used for controlling the body, you should position behind your opponent. If you can't attain the superior position through your own movement, you can often attain it by manipulating your opponent's movement. This is something we will explore in more detail in subsequent chapters.

# Grabbing Exercise

When closing distance, and throughout the takedown, be aware that your opponent has a natural tendency to reach out and grab you. Your opponent's first reaction, when experiencing a loss of balance, is to reach out and grab something to stabilize himself. Pay attention to the position of your arms, neck, or loose clothing, as your opponent will naturally reach for these when he starts to lose balance.

1. Have your partner grab you using a variety of grabs: shoulder, neck, or waist. Avoid "grabbing the hand that grabs you." Your desire to grab him back should be more apparent if he uses a push or pull simultaneous to the grab.

2. When grabbed, experiment with how you can push or pull your partner off balance without grabbing the hand that grabs you. Can you twist out of the grip, simultaneously jerking him forward? Can you grab or push against his body while ignoring his grip on you? How forceful must your push or pull be to solicit a reaction?

3. Observe the weak points on your opponent's arm when he grabs you: the shoulder, elbow, wrist, and finger joints. Can you use a strike or push against his elbow to hurt it enough to make him straighten his arm or loosen his grip?

## Positioning After the Takedown

When you have succeeded at taking your opponent down, consider getting to safety. The most obvious is to turn and run the opposite direction. However, this is not always feasible. Again, you must keep your escape routes in mind. If possible, avoid stepping over your opponent, as this is an opportunity for him to grab or trip you. If you must step over your opponent, consider stepping over his head rather than his feet. If he reaches out and grabs you and succeeds at pulling you down, you can control him by his head easier than by his feet. We will explore this in Chapter 7 on presses.

## Ground Exercise

A fight isn't over until it's over. Although your unbalancing move may have been successful, don't relax until you have distanced yourself enough from the situation that you have eliminated the possibility of a new threat from developing.

1. Have your partner lie on his back on the ground, while you walk past him within grabbing distance. First, walk past his legs. What offensive techniques can he use? Can he kick you? Trip you? Next, walk past his middle. How can he readjust his position so that he still can reach you? Can he pivot on his butt or hip? Next, walk past his head. How easy or difficult is it for your partner to pull you to the ground? Can he turn on his side to facilitate a takedown?

2. If you have to step over or walk past an opponent who is down, what offensive techniques can you use to hurt or stun him? Try kicking or stomping to vulnerable areas of his body: ankle, shin, knee, groin, hip, chest, throat, or head. Your foremost thought should be to get away, so be prepared to run, not stay to see if your kick did any damage.

# Set-Ups and Positioning

Balance may be the most important martial arts concept. Balance enables you to throw a strike or kick with power and accuracy. Or if grappling, balance enables you to keep your foundation. If you can take your opponent's balance, or move so that his momentum throws him off balance, he will be virtually harmless until he regains balance. This all relates to your opponent's physical balance. But his mental balance may be equally important. Disturbing your opponent's mental balance through a fake or distraction, or through intimidation, helps you initiate an attack on his physical balance. The opposite is also true. Disturbing your opponent's physical balance enables you to upset his mental balance, causing his technique to stall.

There are many ways to split your opponent's focus. One is through pain. This is effective, even if the pain doesn't do any physical damage. Any pain that has shock value will serve the purpose. For example, a hard pinch to a soft tissue area: love handles, inside upper arms, inside thighs, and groin. When is the best time to split your opponent's focus? Generally when he is just *beginning* to throw his technique, but before it is extended. Splitting his focus will have the maximum effect when his mind and body are united in the effort of throwing the technique.

A kick can be an effective way to split your opponent's focus, allowing you to close distance. Stick with low kicks to the legs or possibly mid-section. If you kick higher, you risk giving your leg to your opponent. In other words, he can catch it and use the principles of balance manipulation against you. Whether the kick actually makes contact or not is less important, as long as it solicits the intended reaction.

A punch or kick has optimum power only at a specific distance. If you are slightly too far from the target, you lose power, because you lack penetrating force. If you are slightly too close to the target, you also lose power, because you lack extension. Trying to time a punch or kick to an opponent who rushes you is difficult, because there is only one point in time when your strike will have maximum effect. In addition, most people can take a strike at less than maximum power, and throwing a second strike when your opponent is on top of you is almost useless. If you use a strike or kick as defense, you should be the one who decides when to use it. For example, use it as a set-up for your distance closure prior to the takedown, or use it as a softening technique after your distance closure and before manipulating your opponent's balance. In both cases the strike was used offensively to split your opponent's focus and set up another technique. Using a strike defensively; for example, to stop an attack, is much more difficult.

When engaged in sparring in the training hall, you may block quite a few of your opponent's strikes successfully. This is because you know in advance, before you enter into the exercise, that your opponent will try to strike you. But in order to increase your chances of intercepting an attack in a street confrontation, you must be aware of the dangers of the situation some time before it occurs. This is why it benefits you to be "in charge" of the confrontation. Don't allow your adversary to initiate by closing distance. If distance has to close, it is better if you can initiate with the takedown, before he launches his attack. This will split his mind from offense to defense.

**Your Mindset**

**You are the one who decides when to close distance and initiate the takedown.**

Aside from splitting your opponent's focus, kicks are great for getting a feel for distance. When using a kick this way, a straight kick, like the front kick, is better than the side or round house kick. The side kick requires more movement in your body and may place you in an unfavorable position. And the round house kick is not as useful for this particular scenario, as it allows your opponent to close distance inside of the kick's path of power. The front kick can be thrown to the front of your opponent's thigh, or directly to his knee. Not only does this distract him, it also has a tendency to straighten his knee and unbalance him, bringing his upper body forward, and making him cautious of moving closer.

**A kick to the front of your opponent's thigh can have the effect of halting his advance and bringing his upper body forward. This may allow you to escape, rather than pursuing the takedown.**

If you move in without using some kind of set-up first, you will make yourself vulnerable to a counter-attack. Once you have split your opponent's focus, explode forward for the takedown. The takedown itself must be dynamic and happen without any stuttering or stop in momentum. Rely on the moment of surprise. The idea is to have your opponent still thinking about the kick. Stopping the momentum may inadvertently place you in position to be grabbed or taken down.

**The round house kick is not the most effective kick as a set-up for a takedown, because the curved path of the kick allows your opponent to move inside of the kick's path of power.**

When your opponent moves in, your foot, where the greatest linear speed is, will be kicking air behind the target.

Unless you have trained considerably at kicking from close range, the round house kick is strongest at the tip, because this is where the greatest linear speed is. If your opponent moves inside of the curved path of your foot, he can take the kick on his arm without much damage. If you are defending against the round house kick, this bit of knowledge can be used to your advantage. Safety is now in closeness rather than in distance. When your opponent initiates the kick, execute a fast gap closure and take the kick on your arm. You are now at close range and in a superior position for a takedown, with your opponent in a nearly unbalanced stance on one foot. However, if you are throwing a kick as a distraction or to keep your opponent at a distance, a kick following a straight path, like the front kick, is a better technique.

## Action-Reaction Exercise

Having an understanding of cause and effect can help you time your takedown to a weakness in your opponent's position.

1. Face a partner at a distance of approximately five feet. Twitch your body suddenly, or raise your leg suddenly as if to throw a kick. Observe your partner's reaction. Does he respond to your sudden move? Does he have a tendency to move back? Drop his hands?

2. A move without follow-through could be dangerous in a self-defense situation because, after the initial surprise, you are giving your opponent the opportunity to respond. The element of surprise is your window of opportunity. Practice closing the gap immediately and aggressively following your kick.

3. Have your partner hold a kicking shield for protection, or if that's not available, stand with one side of his body and shoulder facing you. Start from a distance of ten feet and run into your partner forcing him to take a step back, no matter what. We have a natural tendency to want to stop our momentum when faced with a barrier, but stopping also gives your opponent the opportunity to regroup and adjust to your gap closure. You must allow your momentum to continue through the target.

**Your Mindset**

**Overwhelm your opponent. Don't trade blows like you would in sports. Think offense.**

## Timing

Before moving in for the takedown, consider your opponent's offensive capabilities. If you are trying to set up the takedown with a kick, but your opponent is also using a kick as a set-up for his technique, you will essentially be meeting power with power. Even though your focus is on taking the active approach, you may now be reluctant to move in for the takedown. Once you start backpedaling, you are giving up any advantage you may have had. Rather than trying to avoid or defeat your opponent's kick, try to take advantage of his timing.

If he is throwing a round house kick, move in when he is in the process of kicking. He is now on one leg, and his mind is absorbed in throwing the kick. If he is throwing a front kick, this is not a good time to move in, however, as you will essentially be walking into the power of the kick. The front kick can be defeated by avoiding it through a step back, and by timing your advance to your opponent's withdrawal of the kick, ideally right before his foot touches the ground.

You can also defeat a kick by reacting to it the moment your opponent initiates the kick. Pay attention to the slightest move or twitching of his body and initiate your move before he has a chance to do his. A third option is to move slightly to the side, preferably toward your opponent's back, and allow the kick to miss. But this requires good timing and is a little more difficult to learn without sufficient practice.

## Timing Exercise

Timing is the ability to take advantage of a pause in your opponent's offense, or a weakness in his position.

1. Initiate your gap closure the moment you see the first twitching in your partner's body, prior to him throwing a kick. Your advance must be quick and explosive in order to take advantage of his moment of weakness.

2. Have your partner throw a kick from a distance of five feet. When the kick misses, he must replant his foot. This is his moment of weakness. Initiate your distance closure the moment you observe his kick miss.

3. Practice carrying your momentum all the way through the target. Use a move you observe in your partner's body, or the initiation of his kick, to trigger your advance. Once you have decided to close distance, don't stop until you have moved your partner at least one foot to the rear.

# Softening Techniques

A softening technique is often necessary prior to a takedown. Even if you have gained the superior position, your opponent will have a lot of adrenaline and will be fighting against you. Giving your opponent a new point of pain can split his focus and enable you to execute the takedown. Throw a series of softening techniques before attempting to unbalance your opponent.

Be aware of the target areas. Go for targets that will do damage or cause pain. Kicks to the legs or knee strikes to the gut can be effective, or execute a series of quick punches to the face. Throw your strikes with intent. Don't allow your opponent to increase the distance between you, or you will be back to where you started. If your opponent backs up, follow with aggressive strikes or kicks. The punches must be quick to avoid getting grabbed or struck back. Kicks should be thrown low to decrease the danger of getting your leg grabbed or of losing your balance. A person who takes four or five strikes in rapid succession has difficulty defending, especially if he doesn't expect you to throw them. The idea is to overwhelm your opponent and quickly go for the takedown.

**A knee to the thigh, a punch to the face, and a kick to the groin can be used as softening techniques if done quickly and with intent. Don't wait for your opponent's reaction. Be furious in your attack.**

**Your Mindset** **Once committed to the takedown, don't allow your momentum to stop until your opponent goes down.**

## Target Areas for Softening Techniques

A softening technique is designed to temporarily weaken your opponent's point of attack, allowing you to escape or close distance for a takedown. Note that many of these targets, when struck, also have the potential to end the fight:

1. The temples can be struck with the back or side of your fist. The temple is the soft spot, about the size of a quarter, at the side of your head and directly in line with your eye. A strike to this area can cause a concussion or blurred vision.

2. The ears can be grabbed and pulled and twisted. A light to moderate open hand slap can shock the eardrum enough for it to rupture. A light slap will create ringing in the ear and a temporary balance disturbance or disorientation, even without a rupture of the eardrum. If you have the opportunity to slap both ears simultaneously, the effect can be severe.

3. The eyes can be penetrated with finger pokes or scratched with a finger whip. As we all know, the eyes are very sensitive to even the slightest touch.

4. The nose can be struck with a regular or vertical punch, or with a palm strike. Many people bleed easily and profusely from the nose when struck, and a nose bleed often looks worse than it is, creating a psychological reaction. Striking the nose also causes the eyes to water.

5. The elbows can be hyper-extended through the push-pull principle, as discussed in Chapter 3. If your opponent's arm is straight, a hard blow to the back of the elbow can hyper-extend the joint. If possible, isolate the joint with the arm in the extended position and utilize opposing forces against the natural movement of the joint.

6. The fingers can be grabbed and bent or twisted against their natural range of motion. Your opponent's hands are your biggest threat. The hands are very fast and mobile, and most every technique an

adversary tries involves some use of his hands. If you damage the hands or fingers, you severely limit your opponent's will to fight.

7. The groin can be kicked or kneed, or grabbed, squeezed, and ripped. The groin is extremely sensitive to contact. Don't discount the female attacker. A forceful kick to the pubic bone creates shocking pain.

8. The legs and knees can be kicked with a side kick, stop kick, or stomp. For the purpose of self-defense, keep all kicks low. The shins and ankles are sensitive to contact, especially if you are wearing shoes with a coarse sole. The knees can be attacked from the front or side. A kick to the side of the knee (either inside or outside) will cause the knee to buckle with possible damage to ligaments.

Softening techniques also involve techniques intended to solicit a pain reaction without doing permanent damage. This includes grabbing and pinching soft tissue areas where sensitive nerves are located. A few examples are inside thighs, inside upper arms, pectorals, neck, and cheeks. The less tissue you grab, the more shock value it has. If you combine a pinch with a forceful twist, you will increase the effectiveness even more. Use pinching techniques when you don't have a lot of room to execute a strike; for example, when your opponent has pinned your arms to your body, or when you are on the ground with him. The sole purpose of the pinch is to open a window of opportunity for you to either escape or continue with a takedown.

## Target Exercise

Strikes can be used to create *sensory overload*, a state of chaos and confusion intended to split your opponent's focus. When used for this purpose, it is not necessarily the targets you strike that are important, but the number of strikes you throw and your ability to strike a variety of targets in rapid succession.

1. Practice combinations of strikes or kicks to different targets in slow motion with a partner. Include strikes to at least two different target areas. For example, a kick to the gut and a strike to the head, or a kick to the knee and a knee to the groin.

2. How forceful must the strikes be in order to be effective? Have your partner hold a kicking shield or focus mitts, and throw your strikes with enough force to make him move at least one inch to the rear.

3. Have your partner start backing up when you throw your first strike. Don't let him get away. Practice staying within range to follow with successive strikes or kicks. If you allow your opponent to gap now, you also give him the opportunity to attack you in the pause between combinations. If your intent is to proceed with a takedown, be ready to stay within range and act quickly once you have split your opponent's focus with softening strikes.

## Your Zone of Safety

When walking from your car to your job, or from your car to the mall, observe others who are walking in the vicinity. Identify your zone of safety. When you have to pass people on the sidewalk, are they close enough to reach out to grab you? Sometimes it is necessary to allow others into your zone of safety, as when passing them in tight quarters. Identify ways to unbalance your opponent. Observe others who are coming toward you from a distance and identify how you would proceed with a takedown, should it be necessary. The purpose of this exercise is to increase your awareness and explore different people's physical builds and how they project themselves mentally, in order to help you determine your best course of action. When a person is moving toward you, how can you move to establish the superior position from the beginning?

Ask yourself frequently, "What would I do if attacked right now?" How would you react, respond, defend, run away? Just asking yourself this question heightens your awareness and makes you less likely to be attacked. It's when the attack is a surprise, when the assailant takes advantage of a lapse in your awareness, that even a trained martial artist may not be successful. Being mentally ready makes you more physically ready. When you are mentally and physically ready, it is easier to respond both to a real attack and to a sparring partner in the martial arts training hall. This is because you know in advance that an attack will follow, even if you don't know exactly what type of attack it is.

Let me relay the following true example: Recently, a man outside of the grocery store asked me if I could help him out with two dollars for gasoline for his car. It was daylight, in the middle of the afternoon, and I had the desire to help, but I was still aware of the situation. When I opened my purse, I made sure he was well beyond reach, that he didn't have any "accomplices" and that I was ready to run or scream if I had to. Had he started to come closer, I would have told him to stay at a distance until I got the money out.

# Awareness Exercise

Awareness may be your most important self-defense skill. When you are aware of what is going on around you, the risk of getting attacked decreases considerably. Not only does awareness help you avoid a situation before it develops, it also communicates to the attacker that you are not an easy victim.

1. Be aware of your surroundings. Next time you walk to your car from a place you frequent often, look around and identify objects in the environment that can be used to trip an opponent: trash cans, low fences, or street curbs.

2. Try not to get trapped with your back against an obstacle. Identify objects in the environment that can restrict your mobility: walls, fences, dead end alleys, parked cars, or corners.

# Common Mistakes

## 1. Failing to take advantage of positioning.

When seeking the superior position, rely on speed and the element of surprise. If your positions are equal, unbalance your opponent first, prior to attempting the takedown, or it will be a matter of your strength against his.

## 2. Delaying the execution of your technique.

Don't give your opponent the opportunity to defeat you through a break in your momentum. Execute your closure dynamically and with full intent. This is especially important if your opponent's position is equally superior to yours.

## 3. Failing to disturb your adversary's focus.

Use some kind of distraction or softening technique before moving to close range for the takedown.

## 4. Allowing your adversary to grapple with you.

This is especially detrimental if up against a bigger opponent. Even if he is not skilled at ground combat, his extra weight will work to his advantage and tire you quickly. Stay mobile, both in preparation for the takedown and during the takedown itself. Whether standing or on the ground, it is difficult to execute a successful hold on a mobile target.

# 3 Leverage and Momentum

Momentum is the product of a person's weight and speed. Trying to stop an adversary in motion takes a great deal of effort, and may be nearly impossible if you are the lighter weight martial artist. If you allow a bigger opponent to bump into you, he is likely to knock you down, because a person moving at a great speed cannot stop on a penny and reverse direction. The greater your opponent's momentum, the more effort it takes to stop it. Trying to stop his momentum first, before executing your unbalancing move, is therefore counter-productive. But if you can redirect his momentum and capitalize on it, you can make the takedown or throw more explosive using less effort. An example is side-stepping your opponent's advance and allowing his momentum to continue past you, while simultaneously engaging him for the takedown. Stepping off the attack line buys you a second or two of time, and may also allow you to flee the situation. This section discusses momentum, both your own and your opponent's, and how to use it to your advantage.

## Lesson Objectives

At the end of this lesson, you should understand:

1. How to use two points of balance and the push-pull principle
2. How to use momentum and the push-pull principle in unison
3. How to increase the effectiveness of a takedown by combining linear and circular motion
4. Why the head is such a good target
5. How to properly direct the energy
6. The benefits of using "first touch" to trigger the takedown

# The Push-Pull Principle

The push-pull principle is a leverage concept designed to divide the workload equally between both sides of your body. In order to utilize this principle, you must first attain *two points of balance*. You must be in contact with two different points on your opponent's body simultaneously, preferably of different height, and with considerable spacing between them. For example:

The elbow and wrist have good spacing between them.

**Leverage is achieved by pulling the wrist toward you, simultaneously pushing against the back of the elbow.**

Pushing on one point and pulling on the other, creates a turning or twisting motion in your opponent's body. Circular momentum is chaotic and difficult to counter, because a person can only resist a move in one direction at a time. For example, if you push straight back on your opponent's chest, he is likely to step to the rear with one foot to brace himself for balance. But if you push on one of his shoulders and pull on the other, starting a rotation in his upper body, you will break his postural alignment, making it nearly impossible for him to brace himself, especially if the move is done suddenly. Because a circle employs a constant change in direction, the push-pull principle makes it difficult for your opponent to focus his power against the technique.

**The chin and back of head have less spacing between them, but is still effective, because of the inherent weakness of the neck.**

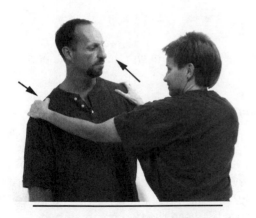 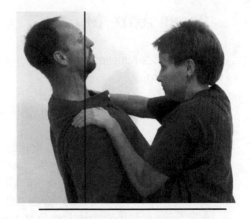

If you start a rotation in your opponent's upper body, he will have difficulty maintaining balance. Use the push-pull principle, pushing with one hand and pulling with the other.

Imagine a vertical pole going through your opponent's body. The quickest rotation is achieved by twisting his body around this pole. As soon as you achieve rotation and break his posture, start an unbalancing move to the rear.

## Two Points of Balance Exercise

When utilizing the two points of balance, you should be in contact with two targets on your opponent's body simultaneously, and use opposing forces of motion to start a rotation around an axis midway between these points.

1. Push lightly against the center of your partner's chest with one hand. Note his tendency to take a step back. Move your hand to the right or left of the center, and push against one of his shoulders. Note how this creates a rotation in his upper body.

2. The push is only *half* of the technique's potential. Place your free hand on your partner's other shoulder and pull, using opposing movement in your hands. Note how this increases the speed of the rotation, making it difficult for him to step with the technique. This is therefore more effective for unbalancing him.

## Lever Arm

The physics concept we will work next relies on the push-pull principle and is called *torque*.

### *Torque = lever arm X force*

Torque is a leverage concept. In layman's terms, this means that the longer the lever arm, the less force you need to apply to produce a given amount of torque, or to move a mass. A long lever arm is beneficial to a smaller or weaker person, who may have difficulty producing a high force. In the push-pull principle, the lever arm is the distance between the two points of balance. The farther apart these points are, the less force you need to unbalance an opponent.

When taking your opponent down to the rear from a superior position behind him, as when coming to the rescue of another person, grab his body at the highest possible point. Since his feet are the pivot point, his whole body (to your point of grip) becomes the lever arm. Grabbing around the forehead is advantageous because the neck is inherently weak, and also because the spine does not naturally bend to the rear. Grabbing around the body in a bear hug makes the takedown more difficult because the lever arm is shorter, and also because it allows the opponent to shift his center of gravity through the use of a natural bend in the body (his waist).

 **It is easy to make the mistake of exercising only one half of the push-pull principle: you push but forget to pull, or vice versa. This is only half as effective, and**

**Think about this** **may not work at all in a takedown.**

When utilizing the push-pull principle, the two points of balance don't necessarily have to be *grabs*. For example, if you grab your opponent with one hand on each of his shoulders, you have two points of balance. But if you grab the heel of his foot with one hand and pull, and place your shoulder against his knee and push, you also have two points of balance. Whenever possible use parts of your body other than your hands in the push-pull principle. This frees up your hands for other tasks.

Grabbing the heel and pushing with your shoulder above the knee utilizes two points of balance. This also frees up your other hand. If your opponent's leg is heavy and you are small, you may need two hands to lift it.

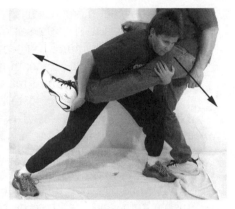

Don't forget that there are many parts of your body, other than your hands, that you can use to achieve leverage. In the picture on the left, both of the forearms are used in the push-pull principle, along with the leg to stabilize the opponent's foundation.

The push-pull principle works both from a standing position and from the ground. Let's look at how to increase the effectiveness of a takedown through proper use of this principle.

## Momentum and the Push-Pull Principle

When your opponent reaches out to grab you, or throws a punch (a punch is more difficult to intercept, because it happens at a greater speed), first try to establish the superior position toward your opponent's back. You do this best by utilizing both your own and your opponent's motion. Rather than stepping toward his back, redirect his arm to spin him with his back slightly toward you. This requires a push against the outside of his arm (pushing against the inside of the arm will spin him the opposite direction). If the push or parry is done with intent, your opponent will spin enough to redirect his momentum away from you. This is a good time to take advantage of his momentum by continuing with an unbalancing technique.

Remember that momentum is your ability to continue motion by keeping your body weight moving in the same direction as your attack. Or, if relying on your opponent's momentum, to keep his body weight moving in a direction that is advantageous to you. Momentum is defined as mass (weight) X velocity (speed). If either of these elements is missing, there will be no momentum. Since nobody is weightless, the defining term becomes velocity (speed). The difference between velocity and speed is that velocity involves direction, while speed simply tells how fast something is traveling. The direction is important so that you don't contradict your own motion. Once you have set yourself or your opponent in motion, you should attempt to continue or intensify that motion in the same direction for as long as possible. Any stop in motion will stop the momentum, and therefore decrease the effectiveness of the takedown. Any leaning or moving in a direction opposite the intended direction will contradict your momentum.

Using your forward momentum against an opponent who is coming toward you means a clash of momentums, with the lighter person getting knocked back or hurt. But using your forward momentum against an opponent whose momentum you have redirected will *intensify* his momentum. When you have established the superior position toward your opponent's back, with him spinning partially away from you, the best time to take advantage of his position is while there is still momentum. Continue to drive your body into your opponent. Don't push with your hands, but use the full strength of your body by pushing with your shoulder, bending your knees, and driving from the legs. Don't bend at the waist, as this may cause your own C.G. to fall outside of your foundation and may also "exhaust" the motion of the technique (once your feet lag behind, you have nothing left to drive forward with). Your momentum helps you take the place of your opponent's center of gravity, and is likely to knock him off balance.

A strike, or an attempted strike or sudden move, can cause your opponent to flinch or shy away, moving the weight of his upper body to the rear. This is your window of opportunity to close distance and initiate the takedown. If your opponent is already slightly off balance, it is easier to proceed with the takedown and allow your momentum to continue in the same direction he is already moving. This also keeps your momentum from clashing with his. When moving toward a bigger opponent, it is mentally difficult to carry your momentum through the obstacle. We have a natural tendency to want to stop when confronted with a barrier. Experiment on a heavy bag or on a partner holding a shield. Run toward him without stopping at the sight of the barrier, with the intent of displacing the space his body occupies with your own.

**Reminder**

**Redirect your opponent's momentum and join momentums with him. This intensifies the total momentum in a direction away from the attack line.**

Let's say that your opponent grabs your wrist. Your natural tendency is to pull away. However, if you want to capitalize on your opponent's momentum, try to move forward rather than back and initiate an unbalancing technique. If he grabs your wrist, he will probably try to pull you toward him. Going with the motion allows you to strengthen the momentum. As you step in, simultaneously push with your free hand up and over on your opponent's chin. His reaction may now be to counter the technique, letting go of your wrist in an attempt to steady himself. This frees your other hand to be used in conjunction with the one on his chin for two points of balance, one high and one low.

**When your opponent grabs your wrist and pulls, go with the motion into an unbalancing technique to his head.**

You can also increase the effectiveness of your technique by narrowing your opponent's base. For example, duck low, grab his foot, and lift up while pushing down on his hip. Since he is on one foot, he will have difficulty adjusting his base underneath his upper body center of gravity, and once the upper body is pushed back, he will fall. The leg acts as a lever, enabling you to use torque to gain a mechanical advantage. Through the use of a long lever arm, you can move the heavier weight of your opponent's body without a great deal of muscular effort. If the lever arm works against the natural movement of the joint, the effectiveness of the technique is even greater. Try this from three different positions. First, face your partner and grab his foot and lift up while pushing his knee straight. Next, do the same technique from a position to the side. Finally, do the same technique from a position to the rear. As you can see, the frontal or lateral positions give you the greatest leverage, while the rear position allows your opponent to bend his knee and shorten the lever arm. This is not to say that the rear position is less superior, but it is important to note when a specific principle has its greatest effect. If you are facing your opponent, grab his leg and raise it forcefully while carrying your momentum forward. You can now throw him several yards away from you.

When lifting your opponent's leg, do not pull up with your arm only, as this requires a lot of strength. Imagine lifting a heavy box from the floor. The best and safest way to lift it is to bend at the knees, keeping the weight close to your body and lifting by straightening your legs. The same principle applies when raising your opponent's leg. Keep it close to your body and lift by straightening your legs. Keep your arms in the same position in relation to your body throughout the initial lift, until it requires separation in order to raise the leg above the horizontal.

## Combining Linear and Circular Motion

Most takedowns are initiated from a standing position. Common errors when attempting takedowns are:

1. Pushing your opponent back, but neglecting to push down
2. Pushing your opponent down, but neglecting to circle

For maximum effect, combine the downward (linear) move with the circular move. This makes the takedown more violent and therefore more difficult for your opponent to counter. Let's start with a body takedown, where you grab both of your opponent's shoulders. One hand (or forearm) pushes against one of his shoulders, while the other hand pulls on his opposite shoulder. Assuming that he does not have time to step with the technique, this starts a rotation in his upper body, with his feet (foundation) lagging behind. If you are hip to hip with your adversary, it will unbalance him. His center of gravity will shift to the side and fall outside of his foundation.

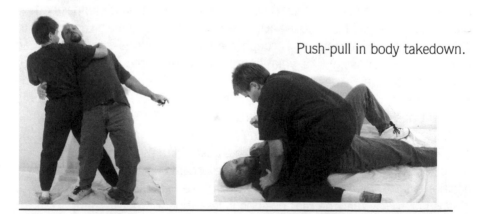

Push-pull in body takedown.

**If you can apply downward motion simultaneously to keeping your opponent from moving his foundation, you will achieve a quicker shift in C.G. making it easier to unbalance a bigger adversary.**

The push-pull can also be used in a single arm takedown. Let's say that your opponent places one hand around your neck in an attempt to control you. To start the takedown, place one hand on his elbow and the other on his wrist and use his arm as a "crank" to free yourself from the grip. This starts a circular motion. Continue pushing on your opponent's elbow while simultaneously pulling on his wrist, directing the energy in a downward spiral motion.

**Push-pull in arm takedown. Note how this technique places you in the superior position behind your opponent. Note also the lock applied to the wrist.**

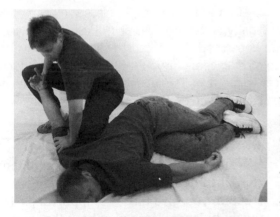

**When your opponent hits the ground, drop a knee onto the back of his shoulder to further control him.**

This book does not specifically examine wrist locks. However, on a side note, a correctly applied joint lock controls more than the joint it is applied to. For example, when you lock your opponent's wrist, you also lock the elbow and shoulder. If the wrist lock isn't applied correctly, your opponent retains mobility in his other joints and increases his chances of escaping the technique.

There are many ways to engage your adversary for a takedown but, by far, the easiest is to unbalance him by controlling his head. Since the head is supported by the neck, which is an inherently weak part of our anatomy, it takes minimum effort to control your opponent by the head. I recommend grabbing his jaw and back of head, rather than pulling on his hair. Use two points of balance, one high and one low. This allows you to take advantage of the push-pull principle to shift the center of gravity. The head is also rather small in comparison to the body, which makes it relatively easy to grab and control.

**Reminder**

**Where the head goes, the body will follow. No matter how muscularly strong your opponent is, he will have difficulty resisting an attack against the head.**

## Head Manipulation Exercise

Head manipulation involves controlling a point of your opponent's anatomy that is inherently weak and well above his center of gravity. If you can lock out the neck, you will simultaneously lock out the entire spine, forcing your opponent to go with the motion of your technique or risk serious spinal injury.

1. Approach your partner from the front and place the palm of your hand against and slightly underneath his chin. Push up on his chin, until his head and upper body are tilted to the rear. He will now begin to feel uncomfortable, and if you push the technique farther, he will lose balance to the rear. This unbalancing move can be done in slow motion and still be successful.

**Be careful not to let go of your opponent's chin until he loses balance. If a gap is created, you give him the opportunity to regain balance. Note also how the foundation is stabilized with your leg. This keeps him from stepping with the technique. Since this is a one-handed technique, your leg creates the second point of balance.**

Note that this is not a palm strike to the chin, but a push with your hand remaining in constant contact with the chin. Speed is of little importance. Try it in slow motion and see that it is still as effective. Although there is a circular arc in the sense that your hand is pushing up and over, this is still considered a linear attack because there is no circular acceleration of momentum around a vertical axis.

2. Approach your partner from the side and place one hand underneath his chin, grabbing his chin firmly between your thumb and index finger. Place your other hand on the back of the upper portion of his head. Tilt his head to the rear by pushing up on his chin and pulling down on the back of his head. Simultaneously start a rotation of his neck with the back of his head toward you. Both your hands should be acting in unison, helping each other, with one hand pushing and the other pulling.

**Circular takedown with control of the head.**

**Where the head goes, the body will follow. Turn your opponent with his back toward you. This gives you the superior position. Continue sweeping your foot to the rear while dropping your opponent to the ground.**

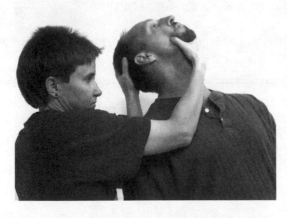

**For maximum effect, use motion around two axes at the same time. Tilt your opponent's head back, simultaneously twisting it to the side to lock out the neck. If the heavier body doesn't follow, severe spinal injury may result.**

Note that both linear and circular takedowns are effective. Which one you use depends on the situation. If you don't have both feet planted, you might have to use a linear takedown.

LEVERAGE AND MOMENTUM

**Your Mindset**

The moment your opponent grabs you, try to gain control of his head.

If your opponent lifts you off your feet, you can still grab his head and push up on his chin forcefully, until his body is arched back far enough for him to lose balance. If nothing else, this serves as a distraction that might create a new window of opportunity for you.

## Safety Tips

1. Avoid jerky moves when working with the neck. Apply pressure smoothly and consistently until you get to the joint's full range of motion. Don't go any farther until your partner tells you he is ready to follow.

2. Ask your partner to cooperate, and make sure he or she knows exactly what the technique entails. Avoid surprises.

3. If your partner tells you a technique hurts or frightens him, respect it and let up on the pressure.

# Direction of Energy

In order to execute the takedown, you must direct your energy properly. If you want your opponent to go down, you must include an element of downward motion in your technique. This sounds obvious, but surprisingly many students fail to do this, with the technique resulting in a push back or a pull around in a circle instead of a takedown. Try these exercises:

1. Start from either a right or left fighting stance. Keep your hands relaxed by your sides and sweep your rear foot back in a wide circle. If you're in a right stance, sweep your left foot in a circle counterclockwise. From a left stance, sweep your right foot in a circle clockwise. Simultaneously lower your center of gravity, as if you were descending a spiral staircase. You are now using a combination of circular momentum and downward motion. To maintain a balanced stance, your feet should be offset at the completion of the technique.

2. Repeat the exercise, but sweep your lead leg instead of your rear leg back in a circle. As you can see, it doesn't really matter which leg you sweep with. How you move depends on the situation, and on whether there are restrictions in space (i.e. a wall behind you).

3. Try the same move with a training partner. Grab your partner's head, placing one hand on his chin and the other on the back of his head. If your opponent is taller than you, bring his head down toward your chest before initiating the circular move. The tighter you keep your opponent to your own body, the easier it is to use circular momentum against him and simultaneously control your own balance. Don't allow your arms to straighten.

Don't allow a gap to form between you and your opponent until he is on the ground.

**Grab your partner's head and repeat the circular takedown. Gradually lower your center of gravity, until your partner is on the ground.**

4. Practice circular motion and direction of energy blindfolded to develop a feel for balance. You can step with either your lead or rear leg, depending on which direction you need to take your opponent.

Note that if you twist your opponent's head *first* and start your circle, and *then* tilt the head back and start to drop, you must change direction from sideways to down. This requires a stop in momentum as you change direction. To avoid this, start the twist and rear head tilt simultaneously, with the takedown resembling a smooth downward spiral with no stop in momentum.

Circular motion can also be used as an avoidance technique to side-step or evade an attack prior to executing a takedown. If possible, intercept your opponent's forward motion and grab his arm, shoulders, or head as you start circling to avoid the attack. If you're not in position to escape, proceed with a takedown, using the momentum your opponent has already started. If you can simultaneously step behind one of his legs, you have the added benefit of keeping him from shifting his lower body center of gravity to regain stability. Keep your own stance wide for better balance.

**Evade the strike and use opponent's forward momentum to throw him off balance.**

Note the push-pull on the elbow and wrist combined with circular motion.

**You can also evade the attack, step to the superior position behind your opponent, and proceed with a rear takedown using circular momentum. Note the two points of balance: the head and the arm.**

# Momentum and First Touch

Momentum is important both when initially closing the gap between you and your opponent, and when actually executing the takedown. The next concept we will discuss is referred to as *first touch*, and should be used as a signal to trigger the takedown. As we have already learned, you can't execute a takedown unless there is physical contact between you and your opponent. When closing distance in preparation for the takedown, allow your momentum to continue, using the moment you first touch your opponent as the "start signal" for the technique. This helps trigger your reflexes so that there is no, or only minimal, slowing of your momentum. For a smaller person against a bigger adversary, it is especially important to keep the motion continuous with no stopping or pausing before or during the takedown.

**Your Mindset**

**The moment you first touch is the start signal for the takedown.**

It is difficult to side-step an attack, unless you see it coming from a distance. However, it is a little easier to redirect an opponent's arm rather than moving your whole body off the attack line, because you won't be working against the inertia of your own body mass. Many attacks involve a strike or grab attempt. Be aware of your zone of safety. If you are outside of your opponent's reach (the length of his arms), he must either take a step forward to grab you, or overextend his center of gravity forward by leaning toward you.

Our physical actions often signal our mental intentions. If your opponent takes a step toward you, it is likely that he will also begin to extend his arm at the same time. He now has momentum going in your direction, giving you the opportunity to intercept his half-extended arm and redirect it. If your opponent overextends his center of gravity toward you (if his feet are lagging behind his body), he is already in a disadvantaged position, and a continuation of his forward momentum will unbalance him. Parrying your opponent's extended arm, or grabbing his wrist and pulling in the direction he is already going, simultaneously side-stepping the attack, keeps his momentum going, but to your advantage. You are now off the attack line, along which his full power and intent are focused, and you have positioned yourself to his outside (slightly behind his back). This is an example of how momentum can work for or against you. As long as you understand its characteristics, momentum is advantageous when you want to increase the force of your attack. But if the target is suddenly removed, your momentum will work against you, because you won't be able to stop and redirect your attack.

**Think about this**

**If your opponent increases your momentum in the direction you are already going, while simultaneously removing the target, it can unbalance you.**

If it is a surprise attack and you don't have the option to initiate the technique, you still want to rely on first touch. Regardless of how the attack is initiated, the moment you feel your opponent's hands or body connect with yours is the signal that triggers the takedown and allows you to take advantage of your opponent's momentum to throw him off balance.

## Momentum and First Touch Exercise

Circumstances are often such that you are under the pressure of an imminent attack before your opponent advances. Your first reaction is therefore likely to be defensive. A natural reaction when faced with a sudden strike or grab attempt is to raise the hands in front of your face in a defensive gesture. This places the attacker in a situation where he must react to your reaction. If he is slightly out of reach, he must overextend himself in order to secure a good grip. This could be your window of opportunity to either get away or start your unbalancing move.

1. Face your partner from a distance of ten feet. Walk toward him at a normal pace, and grab his chin with one hand and the back of his head with the other. Proceed with a circular takedown to the rear. The transition between gap closure and takedown should be smooth with no fumbling or stopping of motion.

2. Have your partner approach you from a variety of angles. *First touch*, the moment you feel his hand anywhere on your body, is the start signal to proceed with either a softening technique or a take-down.

# Common Mistakes

## 1. Failing to direct the energy.

When attempting a takedown, we often have a tendency to push our opponent straight back rather than down, or if relying on circular momentum, to pull in a horizontal circle with no downward motion. You must focus your energy in the direction you want your opponent to go (down).

## 2. Inadvertently reverting to linear motion.

When using circular momentum, the circle should be wide enough to throw your opponent off balance. Sometimes, we become "lazy" with the technique and inadvertently revert back to linear motion.

## 3. Stopping the momentum.

The motion should be continuous regardless of whether you use a linear or circular takedown. Stopping the motion allows your opponent to regain his mental composure or brace for the technique.

## 4. Losing awareness of your surroundings.

When employing circular momentum, be careful not to circle yourself into a trapped position against a wall.

## 5. Reaching for your two points of balance.

If your opponent is tall, bring his head down to your chest. Keep the technique close to your center of gravity and rely on the strength of your body.

# 4 | Leg Takedowns

Now that you have gained an overview of takedowns and the elements involved, let's take a closer look at how to manipulate balance from a variety of positions. We often think of targets as "striking targets." But in a takedown, targets are defined as *the area of your opponent's body that you manipulate to achieve the takedown*. Targets can be high, middle, or low, where high refers to the head, middle to the body (shoulders to waistline, including arms), and low to the legs.

1. Examples of takedowns from the high target area are head manipulation or hair-pull takedowns, using *center of gravity* as the primary principle of balance manipulation.

2. Examples of takedowns from the middle target area are linear or circular body takedowns, using *momentum* as the primary principle of balance manipulation, and attacks on the arms, using leverage or *torque* as the primary principle of balance manipulation.

3. Examples of takedowns from the low target area are single and double leg takedowns, using *momentum* and *torque* as the primary principles of balance manipulation.

In most takedowns, you attack two targets at the same time. For example, if you attack the head, you will probably also attack the body. It is therefore important to understand the three sections of the body, how they work, and how they need to be attacked. When choosing your target, consider the threat your opponent is imposing. Is he striking or reaching out to grab you? Is he kicking you? Is he attacking you from behind in a choke or bear hug?

The leg takedowns discussed in this chapter have the advantage of stealing your opponent's foundation instead of shifting his upper body center of gravity. When the foundation is gone, the heavier body will fall.

## Lesson Objectives

At the end of this lesson, you should understand:

1. How to choose an appropriate target
2. The benefits of manipulating more than one target at a time
3. How to manipulate balance through a leg takedown involving a shoot
4. How to manipulate balance through a leg takedown involving the trapping of a kick
5. How to use your free "weapons" to facilitate the takedown
6. What to do when your opponent hits the ground

# A Conceptual Look at Targets

In stress based self-defense training, the adrenaline is high, and if instruction is too precise (one quarter of an inch above the elbow, for example), it is too difficult for the average student without devoting himself to years of training. This is why I choose to teach the concepts instead of the exact location of the target. For example, when exerting pressure between the small bones of your opponent's hand, you create pain that may distract him enough to allow you to break his grip. But it is less important whether this pressure is applied between the first and second finger or between the second and third. Learning the general concepts enables a student of self-defense to apply his knowledge quicker.

Your force is both a measure of how strong you are, and of your ability to utilize the natural laws of motion, such as momentum and torque. The strength of the target is also crucial. Consider your opponent's physical characteristics along with his positioning. Also consider your own physical characteristics along with the motor skills required for your attack. Whether you are standing or on your back on the ground, one way to fend off an attacker is by keeping your hands and feet staggered. The lead should be used as a check or irritant, with the rear used as your primary weapon. This works both offensively and defensively, and also gives you a back-up. For example, if your opponent grabs your lead hand, you still have your rear hand free, which gives you the option to throw a strike or softening technique prior to attempting the takedown.

We have already established that, in order to execute a takedown, there must be physical contact between you and the opponent. But what if the assailant grabs you, pins your arms along your sides, and lifts you off the ground? If you have no way of grabbing your adversary, then how can you proceed with the takedown? At this point you must consider your opponent's motives. Does he want to place you in his car and kidnap you? Does he want to "calm" you and keep you from hurting him or somebody else? Does he want to throw you to the ground in anger? As long as his arms are wrapped around you, he is not in position to attack you further, and there comes a time when he must let go of you. The moment he lets go should be considered the moment of *first touch*, which should trigger your takedown. If you only have one hand free, you can still steal your opponent's balance, even if he has lifted you off the ground.

## Motives Exercise

In most cases, the attacker has some kind of motive. Being aware of this motive may help you avoid the attack all together, or at least determine an appropriate course of action.

1. Analyze your particular situation in society. Identify who is most likely to grab you. Is it your spouse? A friend? A co-worker? A stranger? What is his motive? Does he want to "quiet your aggressive nature"? Hurt you? Tease or irritate you? Control you?

2. Where is this grab most likely to occur, and what is the final outcome? Does it happen in your home? At work? At a friend's house? Does it result in physical pain? Hurt feelings? Anger?

3. If it has happened in the past, what can you do to preclude it from happening again? Can you tell the person "no" and mean it? Can you stop frequenting the place where it happens? Can you report it to the authorities?

In the following techniques, it is assumed that you have the opportunity to initiate the takedown. In other words, your opponent has not yet grabbed you, so you have both your hands and feet free.

# Shoot and Gap Closure for Lower Leg Takedown

The leg takedown is executed with a gap closure against one or both of your opponent's legs. The *double leg takedown* gives you the greatest chance of unbalancing him. The technique you will use for closing the gap is called a *shoot*. You may set up the shoot with a distracting technique: a strike or finger whip, for example, or by throwing some object at your opponent. When his attention is diverted, immediately close the gap, lower your center of gravity, and wrap your arms around your opponent's lower legs. Your forward momentum should continue until your opponent is on the ground.

**Distract your opponent and *shoot* at his lower legs. Keep your head off to one side. This protects you against a knee strike, intentional or otherwise.**

**Wrap your arms around both of your opponent's legs (preferably), and pull his knees together. This makes his foundation narrow and helps you steal his balance.**

**Continue driving forward, keeping your opponent's legs tight together until he falls on his back. Direct your energy down by tucking your chin toward your chest.**

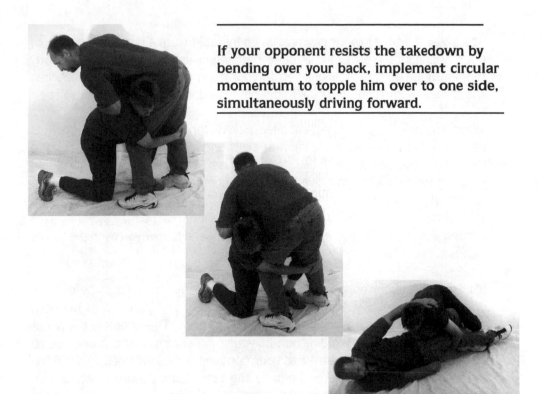

**If your opponent resists the takedown by bending over your back, implement circular momentum to topple him over to one side, simultaneously driving forward.**

Once your opponent hits the ground, you must work into a better position. Don't give him space or the chance to fight back. Preferably get to your feet and run away.

Note that when attempting a joint lock from a stand-up position, the physically weaker fighter is likely to lose. This is because when you get too technical with a technique, you give up valuable time, and a stronger fighter may be able to wiggle out of the hold. Try to get your opponent on the ground first, before attempting a controlling technique, by attacking a larger area of his body and shifting his center of gravity. Once he is on the ground, keep track of where his hands are and, if possible, pin his arms and head. You can then focus on your joint controlling technique. We will look at this in more detail in Chapter 7 on presses.

The double leg takedown is difficult to execute against an opponent who keeps a wide stance. You may now need to resort to the *single leg takedown*. The mechanics for the technique are the same. When closing distance, keep your head slightly off to one side, preferably away from your opponent's free leg. Grab your opponent's heel or calf with one hand and pull, driving your shoulder or chest into his thigh right above his knee joint.

The lower leg takedown is practical when initiated from a distance (outside of your opponent's reach), and is done best when using a great deal of body momentum. Use this technique before your opponent has grabbed you, when the threat is imminent and real, and when you don't have the option to run.

When shooting at your opponent's legs, *drive through* until the takedown is certain. It is easy to get in the habit of executing a skillful shoot, but failing to take the technique to the finish. If you pause (even briefly) when engaging your opponent's legs, you give him the opportunity to resist or negate the takedown. A pause may enable him to bend forward over your back or to sprawl out to counteract the motion of your shoot. Or he may lock his arms around your body, lift you up, or simply sit back and throw you over the top of him.

If possible, set your opponent up so that he is already moving back before you engage him physically. For example, throw a series of punches to his head while taking small steps forward to drive him back. This conceals the shoot and gets him going in the direction of your momentum. You can also set up the takedown with a fake strike to your opponent's face intended to draw the reaction of moving his upper body to the rear. Your closure must happen during this window of opportunity. When your opponent moves his center of gravity away from its natural position, there is a need for his body to correct itself. If he moves his upper body to the rear, he will naturally move it forward again at approximately the same speed. It can therefore be said that the full move takes a two-count. Your attack should preferably happen before his body starts to correct itself. Your momentum is linear the whole time, making this an easier takedown than one that requires a change in momentum. Once you start your advance, continue in the same direction until your opponent goes down.

## Lower Leg Takedown Against a Punch

Fights sometimes originate with punches and escalate to grappling. A good time to initiate the shoot is when your opponent throws a punch. Many untrained people throw wide (haymaker) punches. Work on developing distance awareness, so that you can stay outside of your opponent's reach, yet close enough to counter quickly. Think of it as avoiding his punch, and following it back in with the shoot.

As long as you are in control of your composure, you can proceed with the shoot and takedown even if your opponent's punch lands. This, too, can be thought of as "first touch." Your opponent expects his strike to do damage, and you can in turn expect a slight pause after the punch lands. This is your window of opportunity to explode forward with the shoot and takedown.

**Opponent throws a punch at your head. Avoid the punch by parrying or slipping slightly to the rear. Remember that it takes some time to reset your body's balance.**

**When the strike misses, time your advance to his next strike. The shoot places you below the line of attack. Wrap both arms around his legs and squeeze his knees tight, simultaneously driving forward.**

**Caution: When shooting at your opponent's legs, do not allow both of your knees to touch the ground, as it is difficult to drive forward from this position.**

**Reminder**

**It is important to aim properly when shooting at your opponent's legs. Aiming above the knees makes it more difficult to steal balance. The shoot and takedown should happen in one fluid motion. Baby steps or fidgeting disrupt the momentum and give the technique away.**

## Self-Assessment Composure Exercise

Having an understanding of how you are likely to react to different levels of threat makes it easier to train and prepare for an encounter. Critical self-study and analysis help. Look back at your prior experiences, when you have been in a verbal or physical confrontation.

1. Visualize yourself in a confrontation with a person attacking you verbally at first. If he is a stranger, how will you react? Do you feel the anger building? Will you do whatever you can to distance yourself from the situation?

2. If the person is somebody you know, how does this change your reaction? Does it make you more or less likely to want to argue back?

3. Now, visualize this person taking a step forward, as if to reach out to grab or punch you. Is your first reaction to turn and run? Ask him to stop? Escalate by fighting back?

4. Visualize yourself cornered, so that you can't run. The moment your opponent reaches for you is your window of opportunity. If you delay your shoot and takedown for just a fraction of a second, it may be too late to execute the technique.

## Lower Leg Takedown from the Ground

The lower leg takedown can be executed from a position on the ground with your opponent standing, as might be the case if he has unbalanced you. The same principles apply. Squeeze his knees together to narrow his foundation, and drive forward with your shoulder against his leg right above the knee. Be aware that you are already in a disadvantaged position when on the ground, so it is more difficult to gain momentum or trap a kicking leg than when standing.

**Try not to end up on your butt, as it is almost impossible to gain leverage and momentum from this position.**

**If you are smaller than the opponent and end up on the ground with him, his greater weight will give him the advantage. There is also a danger of being stunned when hitting the ground. This is something you must prepare for mentally.**

## Wide vs. Narrow Separation

The greater the separation between your hands, the easier the push-pull principle is to execute. If you grab your opponent's heel with one hand, and his leg right above the knee with the other hand, you have good separation. But if you place your hand just below his hip (where the leg joins the body), instead of right above the knee, you have greater separation. The hip is also a natural bend in the body, and pushing against it causes your opponent's upper body to come forward. But his leg will remain straight, because you have isolated the knee between your two points of balance. Forcing your opponent to sit when he is unable to bend his leg makes for a hard impact with the ground. So keeping your opponent's leg straight facilitates getting the wind knocked out of him when he lands, with possible injury to his tailbone.

If your arms are long enough to use wide separation comfortably, it is recommended over shorter separation. Pushing with your forearm instead of with your hand makes the technique stronger because of the stronger bones in the forearm, and also because the forearm, when bent, is nearly lined up with the centerline of your body, which is your point of strength. Instead of manipulating your opponent's upper body, you will manipulate his base, causing the heavier body to fall. Because your own position is low when connecting with the leg, it is also more difficult for your opponent to grab you in a counter-attack. This technique lends itself to any attack aimed at your upper body (punch, grab), where you move back and let the attack miss, or parry it and move in for the takedown.

If you have hold of your opponent's foot after he falls, you can use the inherent weakness of the ankle to turn him to the inferior position on his stomach. Again, you are using the push-pull principle. Grab your opponent's toes with one hand and his heel with the other. Start a rotation of his foot along the centerline axis of his leg. If you twist his foot toward the centerline of his body, the pressure will cause him to turn to his stomach. If you twist his foot away from the centerline of his body, the weight of his body precludes him from turning with the technique, and the pressure is likely to break the ankle. If holding onto your opponent's leg after the takedown, you must act immediately, while he is still stunned from the fall. Any delay gives him the opportunity to kick you or pull his leg toward him in an attempt to escape the hold. Be aware that when your opponent is lying on his back and you have control of one of his legs, his groin is open for a softening technique. Another good target is the knee of his other leg. He will most likely plant that foot with the leg bent, exposing the knee. A strong kick to the side of the knee can dislocate it, tear ligaments, or otherwise injure your opponent.

**When your opponent is on his back, and you have control of his leg, his groin is an open target.**

**Another good target may be the knee of his supporting leg.**

## Replacing Your Opponent's C.G. with Your Own

In a leg takedown, "pulling your opponent's leg out from under him" is not the best way to take him down, because his full weight is resting on top of his foundation. Since your heavier body is capable of generating a great deal of momentum, it is important not to limit yourself to pulling on your opponent's foundation only. Rather, think in terms of *replacing his upper body center of gravity with your own*. Your body pushes against his and takes the place of his in space, while his base (feet) are kept from moving or simultaneously pulled toward you.

You can also think in terms of *replacing your opponent's foundation* with your whole body. The knee is an inherent weakness. By using your weight and forward momentum to "throw" yourself against your opponent's knee joint, you can straighten his knee and unbalance him using the side of your body. Most of the shock is absorbed through your shoulder rather than your chest or head. This technique can be done from a frontal or side position. **Be careful when practicing this technique with your partner.**

If using a takedown that requires you to go down or touch the ground with any body part other than your feet, which is often the case in the lower leg takedown, be aware that risking injury is more likely on the street than in the training hall. Although takedowns and throws should be practiced on mats to soften the fall, this may give you a false sense of security. Roll around with your practice partner on hard gravel ground for a few seconds to feel the difference.

**Reminder**
**A takedown on a gravel surface is likely to be hard on your body. Long pants and a long sleeved shirt help protect your knees and elbows.**

## Common Mistakes for Lower Leg Takedowns

### 1. Stopping the momentum.

Once you decide to shoot at your opponent's legs, continue driving forward until he goes down. If you stop the momentum short of a full takedown, you contradict your intent and defeat any advantage you may have had.

### 2. Hurting your head on your opponent's knee.

Keep your head protected by keeping it away from your opponent's centerline. Allow your shoulder to bump into your opponent's leg, with your head off to one side.

### 3. Failing to attack two points of balance.

Using the push-pull principle is important both in the single and double leg takedown. Although your opponent's foundation is very narrow in the double leg takedown, you should still drive your chest or shoulder into his thigh above the knee joint, simultaneously pulling his lower legs toward you.

**4. Failing to initiate balance manipulation prior to the full takedown.**

Make sure you pull your opponent's legs tight together at the knees. If you let him keep some of his balance, he can bend forward over your back or take a step and brace himself.

**5. Stopping the momentum after your opponent goes down.**

Once your opponent hits the ground, it is equally important to continue the momentum until you can get back to your feet, or until you have established superiority away from his natural weapons.

**6. Losing awareness of your opponent's free hands and feet.**

A danger with the single leg takedown is that your opponent's other leg can be used as a weapon against you. Keep your head away from his free leg. If possible, twist your opponent's ankle to turn him to his stomach the moment he hits the ground.

## Trap and Throw to the Rear

Leg takedowns can also be executed against high, medium, or low kicks by catching your opponent's kicking leg. The catch is a little more difficult to pull off than the shoot, because it requires good timing of your gap closure to your opponent's kick. However, it gives you the benefit of retaining your upright position. Whenever possible, initiate the gap closure the moment your opponent initiates his attack. When catching your opponent's kick, you can either *underhook* or *overhook* it (wrapping your arm underneath or over the top of his leg). The most difficult kicks to catch are low kicks, since they require you to drop your hands. A low kick is caught best by wrapping your arm over the top of the leg (overhook), while a high or mid-level kick is caught best by wrapping your arm underneath the leg (underhook). Normally, the technique to use is the one that comes most naturally, but the underhook has a clear advantage that allows you to use the leverage of your body to execute the takedown.

When you have caught your opponent's kick, you have also combined your centers of gravity and base; you are acting as a crutch for your opponent. Be careful not to become dependent on him for support. Your center of gravity must fall above your base, so that if your opponent suddenly moves, you will retain your balance. The faster the support is removed, the harder it is to adjust your center of gravity. Experiment with a partner. Lean on each other,

**Overhook of leg.**          **Underhook of leg with leverage.**

back to back, with your partner relaxing against you. Slowly begin to step away. Note how he has time to regain his balance. The same isn't true if you remove yourself suddenly.

It is unrealistic to think you can go into a fight without getting one bruise or blemish on your body. When closing distance to trap a kick, it is okay to take part of the kick on your arm first, as long as it does not damage any vital areas. If taking a kick on a non-vital body part enables you to get to close range for a takedown, you have accomplished your objective.

Use the *trap and throw* against a mid-level or high kick. As your opponent kicks:

1. Shuffle forward to catch his leg as close to his body as possible. This requires timing. Our natural reaction when seeing a kick is to move back and try to avoid it. But this also places you at a disadvantaged position near the tip of the kick, where most of the power is focused. When your opponent initiates his kick, make an effort to move to close range before he has extended his leg.

   Note that the roundhouse kick is the easiest kick to trap, because you are not moving directly into the kick's path of power. Front or side kicks can be trapped by avoiding the kick first, allowing it to come to full extension, and trapping it the moment your opponent begins to withdraw his leg. This, too, requires timing and determination. A second option is to move in and trap the kick *before* it is extended, when your opponent's knee is high in preparation for the kick. This is also a good time to use your body momentum to simply knock him off balance. When he is on one leg, his foundation is narrow, and maintaining balance is more difficult. If you bump into your opponent forcefully and with full intent just as he is getting ready to kick, he is likely to replant his kicking foot in an attempt to steady himself. Although he may not go down, it may afford you another opportunity to go for a body or head takedown.

**Your Mindset**

**See your opponent's kick not as something to avoid, but as an opportunity to gain a superior position for the takedown. Move to close range the moment he initiates the kick.**

2. Trap your opponent's kick in the crook of your arm. First block the kick with your arm, and immediately underhook his leg. If you step forward before the kicking leg is extended, you will eliminate much of the power in the kick and reduce the risk of injury. This also gives you a strategic advantage by placing you at close range and "in charge" of the fight.

3. Take your opponent down to the rear by raising his leg straight up and simultaneously stepping forward and pushing back. Because he is on one leg, he will have difficulty moving his lower body foundation with his upper body center of gravity, and will lose balance. The longer the lever arm, in this case your opponent's leg (the distance from his hip to the crook of your arm), the easier the takedown. Once you have trapped his leg and started to raise it up, slide your arm closer toward his foot. This extends the lever arm and makes it easier to unbalance him. Because the motion of the technique goes against the natural bend of his knee, he is unable to bend the leg to regain balance.

**Raise your opponent's leg quickly and forcefully to throw him off balance to the rear.**

**Caution:** Don't push your opponent straight back, as this may allow him to hobble on one foot until he gets an opportunity to grab you and brace himself. Direct the energy properly by lifting up on the leg simultaneous to pushing back. If possible, walk forward while raising his leg.

**Your Mindset** Do all moves with force and intent. Not only does this steal your opponent's balance quickly, it also helps you establish a threatening demeanor, communicating to him that you are not to be messed with.

4. You can also take your opponent down by catching the kick, stepping in, and starting a circular rotation in your hips, or by using a sweep or low kick to his supporting leg.

This takedown is a little more difficult, because it requires synchronization between the linear and circular move. If you are not careful, you will give your opponent the opportunity to brace himself by grabbing you.

Use the push-pull principle by pulling your opponent's leg toward you, simultaneously pushing against his upper body as a second point of balance. If you can keep his supporting foot from moving, you can shift his center of gravity quicker. For example, step behind his supporting leg and push with your leg against the back of his knee.

## Trap and Throw to the Front

Note that all the above trap and throw takedowns are "inside" techniques, where you work along your opponent's centerline. Catching the kick and moving to the *outside* of your opponent's leg, proceeding with a circular takedown, is an option that can make for a very hard fall. You will now exert pressure against the outside of your opponent's leg and toward the centerline of his body, which places you in the superior position from the beginning. As long as the leg is held high (at least waist level), a forward takedown is potentially more violent than a rear takedown. When your opponent is on one leg, he doesn't have the option of bending his legs to help cushion the fall. As a result, he has to catch himself on his hands or forearms, which are more fragile than his butt or rounded back. This takedown also gives you a superior position after the fall. Your opponent is already on his stomach, so there is no need to turn him over.

**A forward takedown is potentially very violent, causing a hard fall. A quick rotation of your hips, in conjunction with the push-pull principle against your opponent's leg, will facilitate the takedown.**

Use two points of leverage and the push-pull principle. Facing the same direction as your opponent, pull your opponent's foot, ankle, or lower leg toward you, and push with your other hand or forearm on the side of his knee. Use a rolling motion with your forearm against his leg to start a rotation in his hip, forcing his upper body forward. Simultaneously sweep your outside foot back to create a downward spiral. Do not allow your opponent's leg to bend. The more you can continue the momentum, the harder it is for him to resist the takedown. Pull your opponent's leg outward in the spiral to help shift his center of gravity. Keep his leg in contact with your own body and close to your center of gravity throughout the technique. Don't allow for any separation between your body and your opponent's leg. Keep sweeping your foot in a rearward spiral.

Although catching a kick that comes from the side (like a roundhouse kick) is quite possible without taking a lot of the power, you do need to be aware of that blocking a kick thrown with intent by a person wearing shoes can be quite painful. Even if you move to close range and block your opponent's leg and not the foot, there is a possibility that his foot will still hit your arm or elbow, especially if your arm extends slightly behind your body. As stated earlier, it is okay to take a kick on a non-vital area but, if possible, step in and block at the initiation of the kick, or allow the kick to come to full extension first, while you move to a safe distance. Your window of opportunity is when your opponent's focus is on throwing the kick, or right after it misses, while he is concerned with resetting his body's balance.

# Variations of the Trap and Throw

### Jamming the Momentum

Your opponent throws a roundhouse kick. Before the kick makes contact, step in and jam his momentum. Use the full force of your body weight. Your gap closure must be quick, so this technique only works if you have already perceived a threat before he actually throws the kick. Since your opponent is on one leg in the process of kicking, your advance is likely to cause him to stumble, giving you a window of opportunity for a takedown.

If his kicking leg is still off the ground, catch it in the crook of your arm. When advancing, use the shoulder on the opposite side of your opponent's kicking leg to bump him off balance. This affords you a slightly sideways stance that may help you catch his kick closer to the foot, giving you a longer lever arm. Lift your opponent's leg as high as possible.

If your opponent starts to lose balance and hobbles backward, stay with him by walking forward at a rate faster than he can move back. The same is true if he tries to grab onto you to steady himself. Don't allow him to regain balance.

Grab your opponent's chin with your free hand and tilt his head back and to the side for a circular takedown. Simultaneously step forward and in between his legs.

**You are now attacking three target areas: both legs and the head. Tilting your opponent's head back aids as a distraction and further destroys his balance.**

## The Suction Cup

Another variation and good distraction when trapping and throwing is to place your free hand like a *suction cup* on your opponent's face. Spread your fingers as wide as possible and press his head to the rear until his back is arched toward the ground. When your opponent lands on his back, use your knee (which should be between his legs) to force his free leg to the outside. Don't let go of his other leg.

**The "suction cup" covers your opponent's whole face and is a very annoying technique. Push his head back and over in a smooth, determined arc, simultaneously lifting up on the leg.**

Note that the *suction cup* open hand press to the face works well against any frontal grab or attack, not just a kick. When executing this technique against a punch or grab, grab any part of your opponent's body or clothing, keeping a gap from forming between you. For example, grab your opponent's arm by the elbow with your free hand and pull him toward you, or grab around his waist, as you cover his face with your other hand, bend his neck back, and take him to the ground.

**The *suction cup* works against a variety of grabs, and not just in conjunction with leg takedowns.**

When your opponent goes down, press his head to the side and back, as if to elongate his neck. This places severe stress on his neck, making him unable to strike you back.

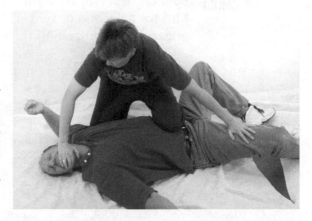

**The neck elongation technique splits your opponent's focus through multiple points of pain.**

## Achieving the Superior Position

If you need to continue on the ground, you can also turn your opponent to his stomach by twisting his foot toward his centerline. Make all moves short, using small circles for quickness and control. Twisting your opponent's foot with his toes to the outside (away from his centerline) causes severe stress on the joint and may break or dislocate the ankle.

**Twist the foot toward the centerline to turn opponent to his stomach.**

**Twist the foot away from the centerline to break the ankle.**

**Think about this**

**When your opponent is off balance, he is momentarily unable to fight back, and in a vulnerable position. The moment he hits the ground is his first opportunity to counter. But impact with the ground is likely to stun him for a second or two. This is your chance to flee or engage in a controlling technique.**

A dynamic takedown has the potential to project your opponent several feet away, especially if there is rotational momentum involved. It may therefore not be practical to follow with a controlling technique on the ground. When escaping the area, be aware of your surroundings, so that you don't escape into a dead end or trapped area. If your opponent is intent on catching you, he will try to get to his feet and pursue the chase. There is also a possibility that he has friends nearby who will help him. The fact that it takes quite a bit of effort to get back up after a fall, especially if it was hard and unexpected, will work to your advantage. If your opponent is in poor cardiovascular shape, it will be difficult for him to pursue the chase after he gets to his feet. Experiment with tiring yourself out with strikes and kicks on the heavy bag for one minute to simulate a fight or struggle. Quickly sit (or fall gently) to the ground, then quickly get back to your feet and run around the room once. Continue with one more minute on the heavy bag. This is supposed to give you an idea of how much a fall, in the midst of a struggle, takes out of you.

## Common Mistakes for the Trap and Throw

### 1. Slow gap closure.

If your timing is off, you will absorb most of the power of the kick before trapping it. Move in and block the kick with your forearm and use the moment of first touch as a cue to trap the leg.

### 2. Failing to use your other "weapons" to aid you with the takedown.

Disturbing your opponent's balance through a softening technique or sweep to his supporting leg will split his focus and make it easier to unbalance him. If you are close enough to push his head back, the technique will be even more effective.

### 3. Failing to direct your energy properly.

Once you have trapped your opponent's leg, there should be no struggle trying to push him down. Remember, if the center of gravity is shifted away from the foundation, a loss of balance is certain. Focus on shifting the center of gravity as quickly and violently as possible.

# 5 | Body and Arm Takedowns

The body takedown is perhaps the most difficult of takedowns for a smaller person to execute against a larger adversary. The reason is that your positioning often ends up being equally superior to your opponent's and, therefore, strength will win. The body takedown must rely on speed and surprise, with your initial attack focused on disturbing your opponent's center of gravity. This gives you the advantage you need to successfully pull off the attack. Because the center of gravity is located in the upper body, and because you are operating so close to this location, it is wise to supplement the body takedown with an attack against the head or arms. This gives you the two points of balance you need to utilize the push-pull principle. Remember from our earlier studies that the farther apart these points are, the longer the lever arm is, and the less force you need in order to disturb your opponent's balance. It is possible to effect a body takedown by attacking two points on your opponent's body (chest and small of back, for example), but if you can spread the distance, so that one of these points is the head or an arm, your takedown will be more effective using less effort. Body takedowns include forward and reverse takedowns with neck or arm manipulation.

## Lesson Objectives

At the end of this lesson, you should understand:

1. How to aim when closing distance for the body takedown, and how the natural bends in the body work
2. The use of gross vs. fine motor skills
3. How to manipulate two target areas in unison
4. Why it is difficult to use straight balance manipulation against the body
5. Circular motion and the benefits of hip rotation
6. How to adapt when the takedown fails

# Closing Distance for the Body Attack

Assuming that you have the opportunity to initiate the attack, distance should be closed in a crouched stance. This gives you the advantage of a low center of gravity. Once you decide to go for the takedown, you must be determined in your attack. It is not enough to tackle your opponent and allow his heavier body to stop your momentum. As soon as you make contact, two points of balance should be manipulated simultaneously. It is helpful to study the natural bends in the body. The hips and waist are the two most obvious. If you allow your opponent's hips to move to the rear, his upper body will come forward, and a shift in center of gravity is more difficult. It is better to immobilize his lower body while forcing his upper body back. If you can add an element of circular motion, you can increase the momentum considerably. Circular momentum allows you to use minimal motion by staying in the center of the circle. A circular takedown employs two circles: the wide sweeping circle of your foot, and the tight circle of your body around its vertical axis. Your opponent should be held as close as possible to your own center of gravity.

It is possible to manipulate the center of gravity straight back and still be successful. The farther apart your two points of balance, the easier it is to take your opponent down. Try closing distance on a slightly diagonal angle, so that you are hip to hip with your opponent, facing opposite directions. Simultaneously push with one hand against his chin (pushing his head and upper body back), and with your other hand against the small of his back (pushing his hips forward). This goes against the natural movement of the joints and is therefore effective for unbalancing him. The two points of balance are the chin and the small of the back, with the hip acting as a stabilizing point.

**A rearward body takedown can be executed by using your opponent's chin and small of back as your two points of balance.**

**Stay close. Don't allow any gap to form between your body and your opponent's. Your greatest strength is along your own centerline. You shouldn't have to reach for your two points of balance. If you are hip to hip with your opponent, you can easily revert to a throw instead of a takedown.**

If you are the physically smaller or weaker fighter, or if you are taken by surprise, you want every advantage you can get. Too much straight momentum results in your opponent moving straight back, where he can brace himself and execute a takedown on you. Proper direction of energy (down) is crucial.

All takedowns don't have to be to the rear. It is possible to take your opponent down forward using a body takedown in combination with an attack on his arm. In the following takedown, your opponent's shoulder acts as one point of balance, and his arm (wrist and elbow) as the second point. This takedown can also be used against an opponent who initiates the attack by approaching you from behind.

**Opponent approaches you from behind. The moment of first touch, when he wraps his arm around you, is a signal to start the takedown.**

**Grab your opponent's arm by the elbow and wrist and start a rotation in your hips. If the technique is done dynamically, utilizing your opponent's momentum, he will be thrown forward over your shoulder.**

Staying one step ahead and controlling your opponent at the moment of first touch, allows you to combine two moves into one. Begin the takedown the moment you first gain control of his arm. When he starts losing balance, he can't use his strength against you. If possible, don't allow your body to separate from his.

## Attacking Your Opponent's Arms

When attacking the arms, refrain from using complicated joint locks that require considerable amount of training and precision. This can be classified as gross vs. fine motor skills. Gross motor skills involve attacks on the larger joints (elbow, shoulder), while fine motor skills involve attacks on the smaller joints (wrist, fingers). Note that when we explore finger manipulation in Chapter 11, our focus is on breaking a grip, and not on intercepting a strike. Although the smaller joints require less movement to cause extreme pain, the larger joints require less precision to intercept in a stressful or chaotic situation. The best takedowns against the joints are those that use the joint itself as a means to take the opponent down. The takedown should not be a struggle. You must know how to attack the joint to achieve the takedown. Any attack that goes against the natural movement of the joint is effective. This means, for example, attacking to the back of the elbow or to the front of the shoulder.

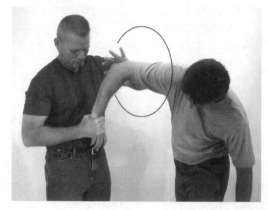

**Attacking to the back of the elbow allows you to use the arm as a crank to unbalance your opponent.**

**Pushing straight down on the elbow straightens the arm. Although painful, this alone does not result in a takedown.**

**The front of the shoulder can be attacked through a "figure four" arm lock.**

**You can also combine an attack on the arm with an attack on the neck.**

As already discussed, the most superior position is behind your opponent. But this position is usually only attained if you are the one initiating with a surprise attack from the rear. However, an attack on the arms can sometimes be used to maneuver your opponent into the inferior position. By using the elbow as a crank, you can turn your opponent with his back toward you, and proceed with a neck or upper body takedown to the rear.

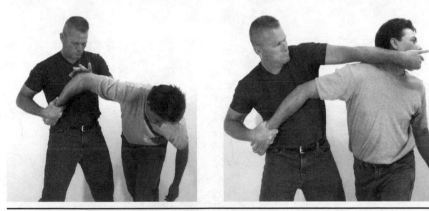

**Use your opponent's arm as a lever against the natural movement of the joint, and turn him with his back toward you. This saves time and energy, and eliminates the need to step to the superior position. Move one hand to his chin for a rear takedown.**

Any time you use opposing forces against two parts of your opponent's body, you will start a rotation. If this rotation goes against his natural stability, it will begin to unbalance him. Controlling the arm simultaneous to controlling the neck increases the effectiveness of the technique by limiting your opponent's mobility. If you control the neck only, there is a possibility that your opponent can turn his whole body and step with the rotation of his neck, taking the pressure off and causing the technique to fail. If you lock his arm in addition to controlling the neck, he will be unable to move his body with the pressure.

In a circular takedown facing your opponent, trapping his arm (preferably around his upper arm to give you the opportunity to use your body weight to its maximum), and tilting your own body to the side (placing more weight on the foot that is on the same side as the trapped arm) helps you start the circle. Any time you can gain access to your opponent's centerline (as when he is reaching out to grab you with one or both hands, or if he has already grabbed you with one hand), you can overhook one of his arms. Note that generally an underhook is stronger than an overhook, because it allows you to lift your opponent up to unbalance him, but it is not always practical against a taller opponent. This is an example of where an overhook works well (see Chapter 4 for photos and description of overhook and underhook). Squeeze your opponent's arm tight to keep him from withdrawing his arm from your grip. An overhook gives you the most control when wrapping your arm all the way around your opponent's arm, so that it forms a 360 degree circle. Use your free hand to manipulate a second point of balance (your opponent's chin, for example). Start a downward spiral with a quick twist of your body to unbalance your opponent.

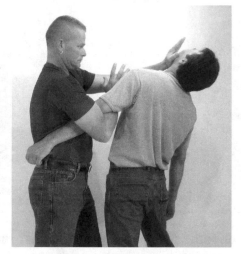

**Rear unbalancing technique with overhook of the arm. Continue your forward momentum until your opponent goes down.**

Whenever overhooking or grabbing your opponent's arm, grabbing at the wrist gives you a longer lever, while grabbing above the elbow gives you more stability. Grabbing above the elbow also keeps your opponent closer to your own center of mass, and therefore gives you a greater feeling of strength. The upper arm also has less relative motion than the wrist. Because it is closer to the body, it is easier to intercept even if your opponent is swinging his arms. The drawbacks are that you must be very close in order to reach his upper arm, and that the size of his upper arm may be too large to afford you a good grip.

# Takedown from the Lock-Up

A lock-up usually occurs prior to a takedown. Your opponent has engaged you and locked one or both hands behind your neck. What is the purpose of such an attack? He might want to wrestle you to the ground, and the neck comprises a good point of leverage. He might want to grab you and pull you along. He might want to control you while continuing with a strike or kick. Or he might want to push you back or steal your balance. If this were a matter of strength, the stronger person would win. The smaller fighter must therefore consider a variety of ways to establish superiority.

**Resisting a full lock-up around the neck is difficult, especially if your opponent uses momentum to move you off balance to the rear, as seen in the second picture.**

Because your opponent's arms are around your neck and he is trying to control you, you can't just step back and free yourself from the hold. Neither can you step forward and gain enough momentum to use your body weight against him. In other words, he is prepared for your resistance, and knows that he has the advantage through his grip. Visualize the technique and try to feel your opponent's motion. Is he pulling you toward him? Pushing away? One thing is clear: he will be using his hands or arms. They are therefore his points of strength, which you want to negate without going directly against the force.

Since you have already learned about leverage and the natural movements of the joints, you also know that the arm is inferior in strength when going directly against the back of the elbow. You also know that if you can keep your opponent from going with the motion of your attack, you are more likely to succeed. Start by placing one hand around his neck to help stabilize his movement. This also gives you a psychological advantage that may split your opponent's focus away from his attack, creating a window of opportunity for you to proceed with the unbalancing move.

By placing your free hand underneath your opponent's elbow and rotating his arm up and over your head, you take advantage of a point of weakness through the use of circular motion. His strength is along his centerline, and you are attacking at an angle perpendicular to his centerline. When you duck under his arm and to the outside of his body, you are in the superior position behind his back.

**From the lock-up, duck under your opponent's arm to the superior position toward his back, simultaneously pushing against his elbow to straighten his arm.**

**Pin his arm against your body, and arch his body back and start to circle. Keep tight control of his arm.**

Keep pushing against the back of your opponent's elbow until his arm is straight. Increase the power through the use of your whole body weight, rather than just your hand. Further stabilize your opponent by moving your free hand to his wrist. This helps you isolate the elbow and use the push-pull principle. Keep your opponent's arm close to your center of mass. Don't allow any gap to form between your bodies.

Place your hands around your opponent's head and cup his chin with the hand that was on his elbow. Forcefully arch his body back. You can also turn his head to the side and away from you, simultaneously applying circular motion and downward pressure to lower him to the ground. It is possible to bring your opponent straight back and down, but circular motion is more chaotic.

Keep your hand on your opponent's chin until he hits the ground. Immediately drop knee onto his head to pin it (we will look at presses in more detail in Chapter 7), or apply further control on his arm. When your opponent hits the ground, your stance should preferably be square to his body (horse stance). This allows you to drop your weight on his head or body, and in general gives you a better position than if you are slightly off center.

Note that when your opponent grabs you, your first concern is safety, and you should try to assume a superior position from the start. By manipulating your opponent's elbow, you turn him with his back toward you. When pulling his chin up and back, you steal his balance as well as his eyesight. Using a sweeping circular motion builds momentum for the takedown, but it is not absolutely necessary. Having shifted your opponent's center of gravity (head back and hips forward), you can simply let go and he will fall. This may be the better option if you have the opportunity to run instead of further subduing him on the ground.

## Variation of Takedown from the Lock-Up

Next, let's look at a variation of the defense against the lock-up. When your opponent locks both hands around your neck, come with both your hands between your opponent's arms and place one hand on his chin (low point), and the other on the back of his head (high point). Tilt his head back to steal his balance to the rear, or turn his head to the side while applying circular motion with your feet and body. Also try this technique by pressing both thumbs into the pressure points under your opponent's chin, tilting his head to the rear.

**This takedown gives you centerline strength and ignores the opponent's grip around your neck.**

The main difference between the next lock-up and the one discussed previously is that you are still in front of your opponent, so your position is less superior. This technique may also be difficult if your opponent has pulled his elbows toward his centerline, in which case you need to go around his arms instead of between them. Still, this technique is easier to apply than the one using elbow leverage. One reason is that it is faster and more direct, giving your opponent less opportunity to resist. Since our common tendency is to fight the arm that grabs us, it is also unlikely that he will expect an attack against his neck. Another strength for you is that your arms remain close to your body throughout the technique.

**Use your body momentum, in conjunction with control of the arm, to trip your opponent.**

**An option is a forward takedown, where you step back while keeping tight control of your opponent's arm, bringing him to his knees. This requires that you go down with him.**

A less common defense against the lock-up around the neck is to place your "outside" hand on your opponent's wrist, and your "inside" hand on his elbow. Now, "bind" his bent arm tight to your body, and use your shoulder or forearm to press down against his shoulder to steal his balance. As he starts going down, step behind him with one foot to immobilize his foundation.

As you can see, separating takedowns into purely leg, body, arm, or head is nearly impossible. For best effect, you have to manipulate more than one area of your opponent's body at a time. The key is disturbing your opponent's balance *first*, before attempting a full takedown. Failing to do this may result in a stronger opponent overpowering you. Second, once your opponent hits the ground, you must immediately flee or pin his head to restrict his use of an offensive technique against you. In a street situation, it is easy to forget those important intermediate steps in the rush of adrenaline. If you start the technique correctly by stealing your opponent's balance, he is unable to counter before he is on the ground and has recovered from the initial shock. A technique isn't finished until it's finished. Think about in advance how far you may need to go, and how to get there safely.

## Takedown from the Figure Four Arm Bar

This technique can be used when your opponent grabs, or is attempting to grab, your shoulder or lapel. Bring your outside hand (the hand on the same side as the grip) over the top of your opponent's arm and into the crook of his elbow. Use your inside hand to peel your opponent's hand off your shoulder. A finger lock may help if he has a strong grip. Fold his arm back into the figure four hold. We will discuss the figure four hold in more detail in Chapter 9. Use body momentum to move your opponent's upper body to the rear with his

**Peel your opponent's arm off your shoulder and fold it into the figure four lock.**

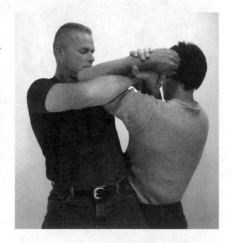

hips forward. Take him straight back and down through the use of the figure four hold, or employ circular motion for a more violent takedown. If you use circular motion, your opponent will land on his side rather than his back. An additional stabilizing technique against his leg can be used to keep him from stepping with the technique.

The most crucial time is right after you peel your opponent's hand off your shoulder, neck, or lapel. You must now ensure that he is off balance to the rear. If his C.G. remains above his foundation, he can use his greater strength to force his arm forward, causing the takedown to fail. Once you have disturbed his balance, however, it is almost impossible for him to resist the takedown. The technique is also quite painful on the shoulder, with the threat of a possible dislocation of the joint. Intensify control by twisting your opponent's elbow slightly toward his centerline. This moves his hand away from his centerline, increasing the pressure on the shoulder.

Once your opponent hits the ground, you need to follow with a controlling technique. The figure four arm bar allows you to keep control on the ground, but requires that you stay very close to your opponent. This technique may therefore be more beneficial during the takedown phase. However, you can use it to turn your opponent to his stomach, and then proceed with a knee press to his head. The knee press is effective when releasing a hold and changing hands.

**Turn your opponent to his stomach and drop a knee press on his head.**

# Takedown as Defense Against a Head Lock

The head lock is another technique in which the leverage of the elbow is useful. You might end up in a head lock when attacked from the rear, as is the case with a surprise attack. Your opponent wraps his arm around the back of your neck, and clasps his hands together at your throat. He applies pressure to your neck by lifting up. The choke happens when the weight of your body pulls the front of your neck down against your opponent's arm.

**Lessen the pressure of the head lock by turning your head toward your opponent's body.**

**Note the control on the hand and elbow.**

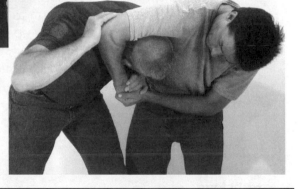

**When you have freed yourself from the head lock, retain control of your opponent's arm and drop him to his knees. Continued pressure and forward motion will take him to his stomach. An option is to let go of his arm and place a forceful kick to his hip or side of body to further unbalance him.**

Escape the head lock by using your opponent's elbow as leverage. Don't fight him at the grip, as this is where his concerted strength is focused. Place one hand on his wrist and one on his elbow, and rotate his arm as if it were a crank. To lessen the pressure, turn your head toward your opponent's body. This makes it more difficult for him to tighten the grip against your Adam's apple or the arteries on the sides of your neck.

If your opponent is very strong and it is difficult to use his elbow as leverage against the head lock, consider splitting his strength-focus first by lowering your center of gravity. Bend at the knees and come back up forcefully, simultaneously executing the technique against his elbow. Since it is not possible to focus our strength in all directions at the same time, this could trick your opponent into resisting your drop in weight. When you come back up, you are going with the motion of your opponent's technique, gaining an opportunity to break free by taking advantage of his momentum.

## Arm Takedown as a Rescue Technique

Since you are not the focus of the opponent's attack when coming to the aid of another person, you have superiority from the start. Whenever possible, a rescue technique should be originated from behind your opponent, where you can rely on the element of surprise.

If your opponent has not yet grabbed the victim, or if he has grabbed with one hand only, you can use his free arm as leverage in the takedown. Approach from behind, cup his wrist, and sweep his arm straight back as close to his centerline as possible. Move his arm until it is vertically straight, and use your free hand to press against his shoulder until he is stooped forward. As long as his arm remains straight and along his centerline, he has to go with the motion of the technique.

**This technique must be done aggressively. Don't fumble with his arm.**

**Note how a step in front of your opponent's leg immobilizes his foundation. However, be aware that it may also allow your opponent to grab your leg.**

Do not lessen the pressure against your opponent's shoulder when he starts going down. Keep his arm straight and through its full range of motion. As you swing his arm to the rear, simultaneously push against the back of his shoulder (where his arm is attached). This allows you to utilize the push-pull principle through two points of balance. Start circular momentum simultaneous to pushing down. If you simply push down or pull on the arm, the opponent can resist the takedown by taking a step. If you use circular momentum, you add a new direction, which increases the chaos and confusion for your opponent. Keep your own body close to your opponent's, with his arm close to your center of gravity. Don't allow for separation between you. Continue the downward pressure against your opponent's shoulder (use your whole body weight). You can also kick his knee as a softening technique. Maintain control of the arm until he is on the ground, where you can either let go or drop your knee onto his head for continued control.

**Use your whole body weight to drop your opponent to the ground.**

The arm can only be moved back so far in an arc to the rear, until the pressure on the shoulder becomes too great. The body will compensate by bending forward, which forces the head down. You can also use your free hand to push down on the back of the opponent's neck, using his straight arm and the pressure against his shoulder to guide him to the ground.

This technique can also be used as defense against a tackle, where your opponent is coming in with his head low and his arms extended. First, side-step the attack, simultaneously intercepting his arm while pushing down on the back of his head to keep the momentum going. Even if you don't get a good grip in his arm, merely side-stepping the tackle and pushing down on his head will throw him off balance, and may afford you the chance to escape. Your opponent's momentum will continue straight forward and down (you will be to the side of the attack line), and it will take him a while to stop his momentum and change direction. An option is side-stepping the attack and giving your opponent a forceful shove to unbalance him.

# Variation of Rear Rescue Technique

As a variation of the rear rescue technique, approach the opponent from behind and bring his head back by cupping his chin with both hands. This exposes his neck and starts to unbalance him to the rear. Wrap one of your arms around his neck in a figure four choke (sleeper hold). Press your elbow down against his sternum while pushing your hips forward and bending your knees. Pressing your elbow into his sternum keeps him from pushing his chin down to protect the arteries in his neck. It also helps you direct the energy properly. Drop with your opponent until you are on your knees in a square stance behind him. Take the choke to completion.

**Unbalance your opponent to the rear and apply a sleeper hold. Drop to the ground with him.**

This same technique can be done without applying the choke. Approach the opponent from behind and bring his head back by cupping his chin with both hands. Slide one hand to the back of his head and start circular motion through the push-pull principle. Direct your energy toward the ground, until your opponent is on his side or stomach.

Whether you choose to apply the choke or just take your opponent down, both techniques start from the same position, and are identical until you have brought your opponent's head back and stolen his balance. You now have the choice of moving directly into the rear choke from the stand-up position, or proceeding with a takedown and then applying a controlling technique. Again, it is difficult to isolate the technique to only one part of your opponent's body. There are several variations of the takedown, but they all work off of the same set of principles. I can't stress enough how important it is to do the techniques with full intent, explosiveness, and no stop in momentum.

# Arm Unbalancing Move from the Ground

Experiment with these arm and neck unbalancing moves both when standing and on the ground. If your opponent is on his knees, you can still use the figure four lock or the elbow crank. If your opponent is on all four, you can still use head manipulation. Because the center of gravity is naturally lower when a person is on the ground, it is also a little easier for him to retain balance. If you start to unbalance your opponent to the rear and he leans forward to counter your attempt, remember that a person can only resist in one direction at a time. Split his focus by implementing circular motion with your knees, rather than your feet, as the pivot points.

**Reminder** Whether you are standing or on the ground, the principles for balance manipulation remain the same, even if your pivot points shift from your feet to your knees.

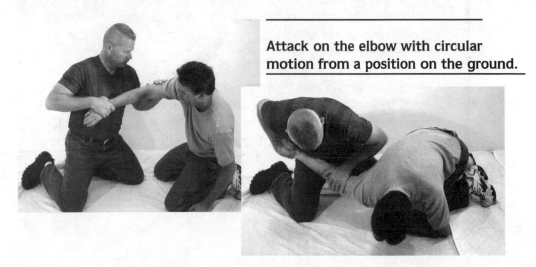

Attack on the elbow with circular motion from a position on the ground.

When applying circular momentum on the ground, the motion of the takedown might be somewhat restricted, because the ground acts as a barrier to movement. When kneeling, stay on the balls of your feet instead of on your insteps and use your knees as pivot points. This keeps your center of gravity forward for stability, and gives you better overall mobility throughout the circle. It also helps you get back to your feet quicker.

**Your Mindset** Be dynamic. Don't allow motion to stop before the unbalancing technique is finished. Don't jeopardize your own position by allowing your opponent to grab your arm, head, or leg.

# Safety Tips

1. When cupping your partner's chin and unbalancing him from behind, allow him to feel the loss of balance first, without taking him all the way down. Once you get used to working together, drop him to the ground while supporting him with your forearms against his back. Be careful not to accelerate the fall by stepping back or slamming your partner to the ground. Give him sufficient time to tuck his chin toward his chest and catch himself on his forearms.

2. When applying the choke, ensure that your partner's Adam's apple is in the crook of your arm to alleviate pressure. The choke could be dangerous if done abruptly and without your partner's knowledge or prior communication.

3. Remember, your partner may not be able to talk when in the choke, so agree on a way to communicate prior to attempting the technique. Respect any signal indicating that your partner wants you to release the hold.

4. When unbalancing your partner through an elbow or shoulder lock, he is limited to one hand for catching himself from the fall. An experienced person knows how to use his whole body when breaking the fall, but this is not the case with a person new to these techniques. Proceed with caution.

# Ground Mobility Exercise

When kneeling, keep your center of gravity as low as possible. If your opponent is taller than you, don't raise up to match his height, as this makes you top-heavy. It is better to bring your opponent down to your level through a set-up strike or joint controlling technique.

1. Kneel with your knees and insteps touching the ground. Have your partner push your upper body straight back until you lose balance. Repeat the exercise, but with your knees and balls of feet touching the ground. Is it easier to retain balance this way? If you rest on your insteps, you risk breaking your foot should you suddenly be pushed to the rear.

2. Kneel with your knees and insteps touching the ground. Now, get to your feet quickly. Repeat the exercise, but with your knees and balls of feet touching the ground. Which position enabled you to get to your feet quicker? This is another reason you want to be on the balls of your feet.

3. Kneel with your knees and balls of feet touching the ground. Plant your hands and practice pivoting on your knees to a new position. When pivoting, raise your feet off the ground, so that only your knees are touching. Do the same exercise without planting your hands. If this were done on an opponent, your hands would be grabbing his head, arm, or body in an attempt to unbalance him.

# If the Takedown Fails

If a takedown turns into a struggle, you need to troubleshoot. Remember the principle of balance: *If the center of gravity does not fall above the foundation, your opponent will lose balance.* There are no exceptions, so your first concern is to shift the center of gravity away from the foundation, which is done easiest by pushing the head back. For example:

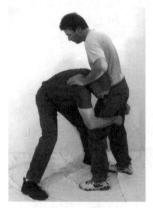 

**If you are tackling your opponent and the takedown fails, shift the center of gravity by pushing up and back on his chin.**

**If an arm crank fails, switch the focus of your attack by pushing up and back on your opponent's chin.**

When practicing these techniques, keep in mind that your training partner is your best source of information regarding the effectiveness of the takedown. Even if he has no martial arts experience, he can still tell you whether he thinks the technique would have worked, had he provided a little resistance. One problem I have found in martial arts practice that teaches takedowns, joint control holds, and throws is that the practice partners are too cooperative, giving you an unrealistic sense of the effectiveness of the technique. You might apply the technique exactly the way it is taught but, because of differences in build, flexibility, pain threshold, strength, etc., there is no guarantee that a technique applied on one person works equally well on another. It is therefore important to take joint control holds to the point of pain, where your partner "taps out" because he *has to* in order to avoid injury, and not because he is *supposed to* tap out at that point. A cooperative partner is necessary to the initial practice of these techniques and concepts, but a partner who gives you a false sense of security can be dangerous if you ever have to use the techniques in real time. Communicate with your partner. Ask him if he thought he could have avoided the takedown or throw if he had wanted to. Ask what he thinks you could have done better. Your partner is the ultimate authority on his body, and can give you many helpful tips on how to intensify the pain and pressure against him.

**Your Mindset**    **Don't continue struggling with a technique that is failing.**

## Common Mistakes

**1. Struggling against your opponent's weight or strength.**

If you have to struggle against your opponent's weight or strength, you are not shifting the center of gravity properly. Your first thought should be to push his upper body to the rear.

**2. Separating yourself from your opponent.**

Don't straighten your arms or allow distance to form between your center of gravity and your opponent's. The closer you keep your opponent to your own body, the easier you can use your momentum against him.

**3. Losing awareness of your opponent's hands.**

Watch for opportunities for your opponent to trap your arms. Remember that you are working very close to him. If he traps your arm under his armpit, for example, he can use the concepts of torque and balance manipulation against you.

128

NECK TAKEDOWNS

# 6 Neck Takedowns

As already stated, the neck is an inherently weak part of our anatomy and, along with its high center of gravity, it is a good point of leverage and an easy target to manipulate. The easiest and most effective neck takedowns involve taking your opponent down to the rear, preferably through circular momentum. The reason a frontal takedown doesn't work well is because when you pull your opponent's head forward, his hips move to the rear, allowing him to retain his center of gravity. If you use circular motion in conjunction with the neck takedown, it is advisable to turn your opponent's head first, until his back is toward you. This helps you establish the superior position. You can also attack an arm simultaneous to the neck.

## Lesson Objectives

At the end of this lesson, you should understand:

1. How to use two points of balance against the neck
2. How to break your opponent's focus when he is resisting
3. The benefits of disturbing your opponent's balance slightly *before* attempting the takedown
4. How to manipulate your opponent's position
5. How to use your stronger leg in an unbalancing technique against the neck from the ground
6. The benefits of executing an unorthodox full Nelson from the front
7. The limitations of the techniques and your surroundings

# Neck Takedown Using Two Points of Balance

Your first thought should be to shift your opponent's center of gravity. You do this easiest by pushing against his chin with the palm of your hand, forcing his head and upper body back. Continue to push until your opponent's upper body is arched to the rear and he is unable to retain balance. He will also momentarily lose his eyesight. Your opponent's first thought is now on regaining balance, making his intended attack on you more difficult to execute.

**Push your opponent's chin up, until his body is arched back. Push far enough that he can no longer retain balance. Just tilting the head, without tilting the upper body, doesn't work.**

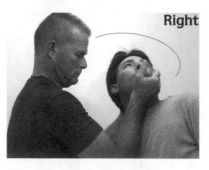
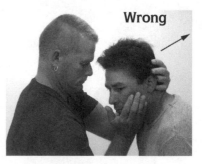

**Right**          **Wrong**

Unless the neck manipulation is done with speed and surprise, your opponent can counter your move by pressing his chin down toward his chest. If he has strong neck muscles, it is fruitless to fight him along the line of power. Because it is only possible to resist in one direction at a time, a quick twist of your opponent's head is usually successful in breaking his focus. Normally, this requires two points of balance. Place your free hand on the back of your opponent's head, using *torque* to turn his head to the side.

**Because it is not possible to resist in all directions simultaneously, this move works well, especially if it is done with speed and surprise.**

**Right**

**Wrong**

**Your Mindset**

**Don't fight your opponent at the point of resistance. If it turns into a struggle, change the direction of the attack to break his focus and strength.**

Using the push-pull principle, with your hands working in unison to share the workload, allows you to twist the neck to a greater degree than if using only one hand. Grab your opponent's chin tightly. A good grip gives you a psychological advantage over your opponent. Keep your arms bent and close to your own center of gravity, using the mass of your body to do the work. The natural range of the neck (side to side, and up and down) can be shortened by applying pressure in two directions simultaneously. Most people are pretty flexible if you only turn their head until it won't turn more, or if you only tilt it back through its full range of motion. But if you turn and tilt at the same time, the range of motion is reduced greatly, making it easier and quicker to establish control. In addition, it places your opponent in an uncomfortable position with his head tilted to the rear. Once you start the takedown, don't let up on the pressure on the neck. Keep the neck at its full range of motion in the side and back position until your opponent goes down.

Note that control is gained by twisting a joint around two axes simultaneously. If you rotate your opponent's head around a vertical axis only, he can step with the motion of the technique and retain balance. But if you tilt the head simultaneous to rotating it, the motion will be a downward spiral, with the result of locking your opponent's whole spine, forcing him to go down or risk serious injury.

The hand on the back of your opponent's head can be substituted for a push against the small of his back. Again, you are using two points of balance: one high and one low. Once your opponent's body is bent backwards, he will be unable to retain balance. Although he may lose balance and fall without any further assistance, be careful not to let go of your control until the takedown is certain.

If your opponent is tall, pull his head down to your chest simultaneous to starting the twisting motion of his neck. The circle should come from the center of your body and not from your arms alone. Your opponent's head merely follows the motion of your body. Pretend that the head is detached from the body, and that you are simply holding it in your hands while pivoting your body in a circle. Remember, where the head goes, the body will follow.

# Safety Tips

1. Use continuous and smooth motion when working with the neck. Avoid quick or jerky moves.

2. Use caution when combining the neck tilt with a twisting motion. If your partner can't move his body with the pressure, spinal injury may result.

3. Allow your partner to cooperate and step with the technique until he gets a feel for how to break the fall.

## Rear Neck Tilt Takedown

As we discussed briefly in Chapter 5, this takedown can be used as a rescue technique when coming to the aid of a friend. When tilting your opponent's head back, the center of gravity is moved outside of the base quickly. This is because the spine isn't very flexible to the rear. If the opponent steps back to widen his base, the takedown will not happen as quickly. But this is not that common, as his focus is probably forward to start with; he does not expect to have to retreat. Intensify the takedown by immobilizing your opponent's base with your feet, by kicking to the back of his knee joint, or by kneeing to the small of his back simultaneous with the rear neck tilt. When your opponent begins to fall, step to the side and out of the way to avoid him falling on top of you.

**Attack the natural bends in the body simultaneous with the neck. The back of the knee or the small of the back may be a good target.**

After cupping your opponent's chin with both hands, keep your elbows tight along your centerline where your strength is. Resting your forearms against his upper back gives you a mechanical advantage. Think of it as pulling with your elbows straight in toward the center of your body. This creates a push-pull effect: your forearms are pushing against your opponent's back, while your hands are pulling on his chin. The workload should be evenly divided between your hands and forearms.

Continue with the takedown immediately after making contact with your opponent. Pausing or stopping the momentum will alert your opponent of your intentions. Act with intent from start to finish. Your combined center of gravity falls within your combined base, but once the support is removed, your opponent will fall. This takedown takes very little strength when done correctly.

The rear neck tilt takedown can also be done from a frontal or lateral position, moving into a rear position. Remember, the superior position is established by stepping or circling your opponent, or by moving your opponent to the inferior position, as when redirecting a strike or kick that turns him partially away from you. If blocking or parrying a strike, stay in contact with your opponent's arm, letting it guide your hands up to his chin. This also serves as a check against his counter strikes. Too much separation between you makes it difficult to close distance for the takedown.

The same technique can be used to parry and side-step a kick that comes straight toward you, or any other linear attack that allows you to establish a position toward your opponent's back. Try it against a downward swing with a knife or stick, or duck a punch and weave to the outside of the opponent's arm.

---

## Safety Tips

1. Be careful when using the knee to your partner's back or tail-bone. Even light contact to the spine can cause bruising or lasting pain.

2. Practice the technique in slow motion and with your partner's full knowledge.

# Defense Against Wrist, Shoulder or Waist Grab

Consider using body parts other than the head for your two points of balance. As discussed earlier, the farther apart these points are, the easier it is to use leverage to your advantage. One of your opponent's arms can be used in conjunction with neck manipulation. For example, if you have the opportunity to grab his wrist in a cross wrist grab, the technique can initially be used to stun and unbalance him forward by jerking his arm across your body. His mind will be on trying to regain his balance. Because his body is turned with his back slightly toward you, you have established superiority and a good position from where to proceed with the neck takedown.

**When possible, disturb your opponent's balance prior to attempting the takedown. This has a psychological effect that is likely to halt his attack.**

**A quick jerk on the arm will unbalance your opponent, split his focus, and place him closer to your center of gravity, which is your strength and balance point.**

When you have unbalanced your opponent forward, reach across his shoulder, around his head with your free hand, and grab his chin. Tilt his head back and to the side and start the circular sweeping motion of your leg (as previously learned) to build momentum. Gradually lower your center of gravity, making sure that your own body is in the center of the circle, nearly upright, and rotating around its vertical axis. Your opponent will land on his side or, if there is enough turn in his neck, on his stomach. An opponent on his stomach is a lesser threat than one on his back. When he lands, you should still be controlling his arm, as this gives you the option of applying a joint controlling technique.

**Reach around your opponent's head and grab his chin. Proceed with the takedown, using circular momentum.**

Note that when executing the above takedown, it is important to keep your opponent's body as close as possible to yours. Any gap between you makes it more difficult to start the rotation. Keeping your opponent close throughout the takedown ensures that he lands right by your feet. This position lends itself to a knee press, which we will discuss in the next chapter.

The same principle can be used against an opponent who reaches out to grab your shoulder or waist. Parry his hand away from your shoulder and step straight in with an unbalancing move along his centerline. Or push his arm toward his centerline, so that his body turns with his back slightly toward you, and proceed with an unbalancing move to his head. This gives you superiority, because your opponent is already close to losing balance, or at least his focus is split. You may also be able to disturb both your opponent's balance and focus by ignoring the grab altogether, and simply placing your hand like a "suction cup" on his face. Make sure to spread your fingers wide, so that your hand covers his whole face. Proceed by directing your energy down. You must arch your opponent's back in order to move his center of gravity away from his foundation. Keep stepping forward with the technique until he goes down.

## Conservation of Energy

When faced with a street situation, positioning should always be kept in mind. A superior position restricts your opponent's fighting ability and betters your own. The best position is generally behind your opponent's back. You can either utilize your own motion by stepping to the superior position, or you can utilize your opponent's motion to help you achieve the superior position. For example, when grabbing your opponent's wrist, simultaneously step to the side and grab his chin with your free hand (your own motion), or pull on his arm to disturb his balance and turn him to an inferior position with his back toward you (your opponent's motion). Utilizing your opponent's motion is preferable, because it helps you conserve energy and stay in better control of the situation.

**Your Mindset**    **Use your opponent's motion to achieve the superior position.**

When facing your opponent, trying to walk around his back is usually a mistake, as it is too obvious, giving him enough time to adjust his position for a counter-attack. Since the neck is an inherent weakness, you can easily turn your opponent's head to the side by his chin. When the pressure on the neck becomes sufficient, the rest of his body will follow until his back is turned toward you.

**Your Mindset** **Use the inherent weakness of the neck to achieve the superior position.**

## Conservation of Energy Exercise

In general, you can conserve energy by using as little motion as possible. If you can get your opponent to position himself for you, your own moves can be shortened and, therefore, quicker, using less energy.

1. Face your partner from a distance of approximately five feet. Try to move behind his back, while he tries to keep you from doing so. As you can see, it is not easy to establish the superior position through your movement alone.

2. Next, grab your partner's wrist in a cross wrist grab. If you are facing each other, you will grab his right wrist with your right hand, or his left wrist with your left hand. Which wrist you grab depends on which side is closest and most accessible to you. Pull his arm quickly and forcefully across your body. If you grab with your left hand, pull across your centerline and toward the left side of your body. Pay attention to how your partner reacts. Is his head near your own center of gravity and in a position to be grabbed? Is his back turned slightly toward you?

3. Next, face your partner and grab his chin with one hand. Make sure your grip is forceful. Even if the grip isn't enough to subdue your opponent, a strong grip communicates determination, giving you a mental edge. Turn your partner's head as far as you can without allowing him to move his feet. If you continue turning his head, the inherent weakness of his neck will force him to step in the direction of the force, placing him with his back toward you.

# Neck Takedown from a Position on Your Back

An unbalancing move against the neck is a good way to reverse positions with an opponent who is straddling you (or is between your legs) from a position on the ground. The same principles apply, with the exception that you don't have the luxury of utilizing a lot of circular momentum. Pushing up on your opponent's chin forcefully will bend his head and upper body back. However, be careful not to rely on linear motion only. If you allow your arms to straighten, you will eventually "exhaust" the motion of the technique and be unable to push farther. Although you have momentarily stalled the attack, it is unlikely that this will finish the fight. In order to get your opponent off of you, you must also rely on a rotation of his head. Use two points of balance by placing one hand on his chin, and the other on the back of his head. Once you have pushed his head back and turned it to the side, direct the energy toward the ground by raising your buttocks and pushing one of your hips into your opponent. All these moves should be done in unison. Your opponent will now topple over on his side.

**Use a combination of straight and linear moves. Use two points of balance, the chin and back of head, simultaneous to a turning motion in your body.**

**Unbalancing your opponent is only the first stage. In a high risk attack on the ground, you must take immediate action to escape or further subdue him until help arrives.**

**Reminder**

Because of the proximity of your legs to your opponent's head from a ground position, don't discount the greater strength of your legs. If your opponent is between your legs, bring one leg up and around the front of his neck, until your calf is resting against the side of his neck. Forcefully apply downward pressure while raising one of your hips off the ground. This unbalances your opponent to the side. If you can grab one of his arms, you can proceed with a breaking technique against the elbow.

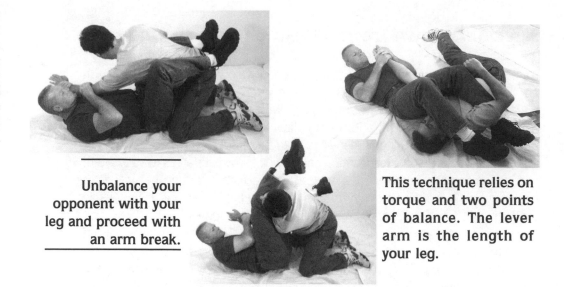

**Unbalance your opponent with your leg and proceed with an arm break.**

**This technique relies on torque and two points of balance. The lever arm is the length of your leg.**

It is likely that your opponent's hands will be close to your face when on the ground. Try to grab one of his arms and pull him off balance forward. This will momentarily distract him and also give you the leverage you need for the unbalancing move. The arm break is done by placing your opponent's elbow against your leg, and raising your hips simultaneous to pulling down on his wrist. This goes against the natural movement of the elbow joint, and is therefore an effective breaking technique.

It is difficult to get to your feet quickly from a position on your back. The unbalancing move by itself may therefore not ensure your safety. An additional incapacitating technique (like and arm break or eye poke) may now be necessary. We would like to think that our goal is to ensure our safety with minimum harm to the opponent, but the time to question the morality of a technique is not when your own life or well-being is at stake. The worst time to work out a game plan is in the middle of a struggle. Think about beforehand how far you are willing to go in order to save your own life, so that you don't have to battle with the decision later.

Note that grabbing or pulling an opponent close, as is often necessary in order to execute a takedown, may seem repulsive especially in a rape scenario. I suggest engaging in physical training with somebody you know and trust in order to get used to working in close proximity to a bigger person. The uglier and dirtier he is, or the more he stinks from a hangover from the previous night, the better. Also engage in mental training exercises. Run through the possible scenario in your mind hundreds of times. Is your first reaction one of fear and repulsion? How can you overcome this and do what is necessary to save your own life?

# Full Nelson from the Front

The full Nelson is used mostly in a stand-up position and preparatory to a takedown. In a self-defense situation, the full Nelson can be used successfully from the front rather than the rear. Face your opponent and bring your arms underneath his armpits with your hands cupping his face. Force his head back and steal both his balance and eyesight.

**The full Nelson from the front is an unorthodox move that can be used in conjunction with neck manipulation.**

From a position on the ground, use the full Nelson from the front to get your opponent from a kneeling position and onto his back. Or if you are on your back with your opponent straddling you, use the technique to get him off of you. Applying frontal pressure against the face bends his head to the rear and arches his back to the point of pain. It also raises his center of gravity so that you can unbalance him easier.

**The full Nelson from the front against a kneeling opponent is more difficult to pull off when your opponent is on all four with his weight forward.**

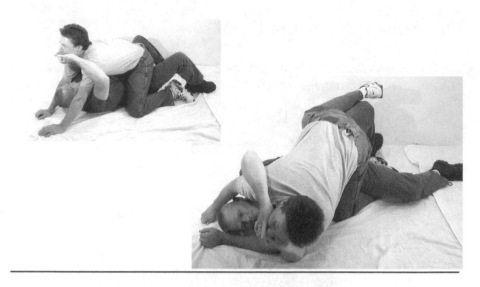

**The full Nelson from the front against an opponent who is straddling you can be executed by raising your upper body with the attack to avoid "exhausting" the motion. Use your opponent's momentum to roll with him and reverse positions.**

Note that when you "exhaust" the motion, it means that you are unable to move any farther. For example, if your arms are straight and you are unable to move your upper body forward, you are also unable to push any farther, no matter how hard you try. Another way to think of this is that you can't exhale before you have inhaled. When you blow all the air from your lungs, you are unable to blow any more until you have first inhaled. Exhausting the motion of a technique, whether physically or mentally, places you in a severely limited position. Keeping this from happening allows you to have an "afterburner" ready when that extra push is needed to save the situation.

## Your Window of Opportunity

Head manipulation defense can be used against a variety of attacks, including a hooking strike or kick, a neck grab, or a bear hug. When your opponent attacks, your first concern is to defend by avoiding or blocking the blows. Use the first touch principle as a signal to engage the opponent for the takedown. This is your window of opportunity. When the attack fails, your opponent needs a second to reset his body's balance before launching a new attack. You have defended against the initial attack, and taken advantage of a weakness in his defense.

If your opponent grabs you from the front with one or both hands around the neck and pulls you close, go with the motion and bring your hands up along his centerline (the space between his arms). If you have conditioned your mind beforehand, it is easier to ignore the natural tendency to resist or grab the arm that grabs you. Instead of focusing on your opponent's strength, focus on where he is *not* strong.

Finally, if your opponent grabs you in a front bear hug, both his arms are tied up, while both your arms (hopefully) are free. Start an unbalancing move by pushing up on his chin forcefully, tilting his head to the rear. Push his head through its full range of motion, until his center of gravity has shifted to the rear. Note that when your opponent grabs you in the front bear hug and pulls your hips toward him, your body is tilted slightly to the rear, making it more difficult to maintain good positioning for the takedown. However, this technique gives you an option, and can also be done if your opponent has lifted you to where you are no longer in contact with the ground.

## Uneven Surfaces

Try unbalancing moves on uneven and tilted surfaces, hills, steps, loose gravel, sand, etc. Consider the weather and your footing. Is it snowing? Is the ground slippery? Is it to your advantage or disadvantage?

In which direction is your opponent most likely to lose balance? Trying to run or unbalance your opponent on an uneven or soft surface is more tiring than in the training hall, and a technique you have done a hundred times may feel completely different on a tilted or uneven surface. The idea is to discover what is possible for you to do, and what your limitations are. For example, it is easy to state that you should be able to take your adversary down when in a confined area, such as a hallway or stairwell, quite another to discover what happens when you try. While being successful is ideal, it doesn't mean that you will pull it off flawlessly. The purpose of these exercises is not necessarily to make you succeed every time, but to give you insight into the situation and the problems you might encounter. It will also make you more aware of your surroundings. Getting caught when on uneven ground can make it more difficult to defend yourself — *or it can make it easier* — and success may depend on how great your understanding of the situation is.

## Common Mistakes

**1. Failing to break your opponent's strength and shift the direction of the attack.**

If you attempt to push the head back, and he resists, momentarily shift your focus by applying a quick twisting motion of his neck.

**2. Limiting your attack to the neck.**

Take into account that targets other than the neck can initially be used to unbalance your opponent. For example, if he reaches out and grabs you, use his arm to pull him off balance prior to attacking his neck.

**3. Not understanding the importance of positioning.**

Know how to use your opponent's motion to place him in the inferior position. The less you have to move, the more stable and in control of the situation you will be.

**4. Discounting the use of your legs.**

Keep in mind that your legs or any other unorthodox technique, such as the full Nelson from the front, can aid you with the takedown.

# 7 Empty Hand and Weapon Presses

The purpose of a press is to solicit a reaction or control your opponent through pain compliance. Presses can be applied empty handed or with a weapon (a stick, for example, or other object found in the environment). The benefits of using a weapon are that you can cover a larger area than with your hand, and that a weapon lacks sensitivity. The harder and less flexible the weapon and target are, the more effective the press is. Look for "bony" targets on your opponent's body. A few examples are knuckles on hands and feet, ulna bones on wrists, ankle bones, shin bones, hip bones, collar bones, jaw bones, bridge of nose, and eyebrows. Certain soft targets are also excellent for pain compliance.

If target precision seems difficult to achieve, apply the press in a "kneading" motion against the general target area. If using a stick, press it firmly against the target and roll it (an inch) up and down while exerting continuous pressure. If using your hand, elbow, or shin, press it firmly against the target and knead in a rolling or small circular motion.

## Lesson Objectives

At the end of this lesson, you should understand:

1. How to find soft and hard targets on your opponent's body
2. How to use empty hand and weapon presses
3. What is meant by the "no sensitivity" principle, and how to use it when striking or blocking with a stick
4. The strengths and weaknesses of different holds on the stick
5. How to immobilize the target when standing
6. How to immobilize the target when on the ground
7. How to use thumb and body elongation presses

# Empty Hand Presses

There are several parts of your body that can be used as a press, including the elbow, heel of palm, knee, shin, forearm, and even the chin if close enough to your opponent. The more of your body weight you can place directly behind the press, and the smaller the area of the press, the greater the force per square inch. However, the forearms or shins, although larger than elbows and knuckles, help you control a larger area without sliding off. Let's talk about the elbow press first.

Most people think of the elbow as solely a striking weapon, but it is also an excellent press or pain compliance weapon. Because of the small and hard anatomy of the elbow, it has the ability to focus the power into a point. Experiment with a partner by pushing your elbow into different soft and hard targets on his body. If he struggles, use a kneading motion. Even with very little pressure, the feeling is uncomfortable to the point that most people can't stand it.

The elbow is a good weapon to use against the mid-section, which is one of the bigger targets. The sides of the body, just below the lower ribs, are sensitive to pressure. Test this by having your partner dig his elbow into your side. A stick can also be used as a press against the sides of the body. First, wrap the stick around your opponent's body, gripping it at each end. Pull it tight against the soft area just below the rib cage. If he struggles, knead or roll the stick slightly up into his lower ribs, and then back down into the soft tissue areas. We will talk more about stick presses later in this chapter.

Your knuckles, both on your fingers and hand, also make good presses, especially if you employ a rolling or rocking motion. Make a fist and knead it into the soft areas of your opponent's body. Experiment with the soft areas around the abdomen, the lower and upper ribs, the sides of the body, and the sternum. Tell your partner not to move. The moment he moves, knead your knuckles hard into his body and again tell him to remain still. Experiment with how much pressure it takes to get compliance. Note that presses are more effective if you can stabilize the target against a wall or the ground.

Sometimes, it is necessary to keep continuous pressure on the opponent's body, so that he is in constant pain until help arrives. If your attention lapses for just a second, and you let up on the pressure, he may seize the opportunity and counter your technique. Once you have achieved a good press, don't give your opponent the opportunity to get out of it. As long as the pressure is present, it gives you a psychological advantage and serves as a reminder to your opponent that you are alert and in control.

# The Chin Press

The chin can be used to press against the sternum, philtrum (upper lip just below the nose), bridge of nose, or temple. This press is most effective in a grappling situation that requires very close contact with your opponent, or any situation where your opponent has trapped you against his own body with you facing him. This is true whether he is standing or on the ground, or whether he is carrying you or not. The chin press may be a good alternative when your hands are pinned.

**The chin press can be used with a kneading motion, much like the elbow.**

If your opponent is carrying you with your arms pinned alongside your body, remember that his hands are also tied up in the technique, keeping him from using them against you. Regardless of where your head is in relation to his, press your chin forcefully into any bony area of your opponent's body: sternum or collar bone, for example. If your head is even with his, press your chin into his philtrum, bridge of nose, or eyeball. Press hard and use a kneading motion to intensify the pain. Even if this doesn't hurt him enough to end the assault, it will break his focus, and may afford you the opportunity to proceed with an unbalancing technique.

# The Heel Press

Because of their relatively small surface areas, the heel or ball of foot may seem like good weapons for pressing. But it is often difficult to place the weight of your body behind a heel press, especially if you are on the ground with your opponent. Standing also has its drawbacks, with your center of gravity high, and a loss of balance brought about easier. However, if you have some way of stabilizing yourself, pressing your heel against your opponent's head when he is on the ground and you are standing can be effective. Note that if you are wearing boots with a coarse sole, a foot press to your opponent's head is more severe than if you are wearing lighter weight shoes.

If your opponent is on his side or stomach, place one leg behind him to keep him from moving, and pressure the heel of your other foot into his nose or face. Use your legs in a push-pull scissored motion. It is a good idea to control your opponent's arm as well to prevent him from grabbing your leg and unbalancing you. Also look for opportunities to use a fence or wall as a stabilizer against an opponent on the ground, while pressing your heel straight into his face. If he is lying with his back to the fence or wall, his body can't move with the pressure, and the technique will have an immediate effect.

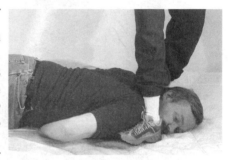

**When the opponent is on the ground, a standing heel press to his jaw, mouth, nose, or eyes might work. Note: this is a potentially unstable stance because your legs are crossed. Dropping your knee onto your opponent's head, or running away, may be better options.**

## The Knee Press

The knee press might be the most widely used press in a takedown situation. The knee press is designed to trap various parts of your opponent's body from a position on the ground. Apply the knee press by placing your entire body weight above your knee or shin, and pressing against your opponent's head, arms, legs, or body.

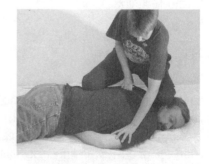

**The knee press to the head gives you good control on the ground. Put as much body weight as possible into the press. Note how the opponent's arm is trapped under his body. Also note the kneading knuckle press against the spine.**

If your opponent struggles, consider striking in conjunction with pressing. When your opponent's head is in contact with the ground, a strike to the head is devastating because the target can't move with the force.

# Target Exercise

When your opponent grabs you, rather than fighting him at the grip where his concerted strength is, place a finger, fist, elbow, or palm heel against any bony area within reach (wrist, collar bone, nose) and exert pressure in a kneading motion. This may solicit a reaction that makes him lessen his grip long enough for you to escape, attain a superior position, or execute an unbalancing technique.

1. Using care, experiment on a partner to determine the best target for a pain compliance press.

2. Have your partner execute a variety of grabs (bear hug, wrist grab, choke, etc.) Identify presses that can be used against the bony areas of your opponent's body to make him loosen his grip.

3. Face your partner from a position on the ground, and experiment with presses that split his mind and body focus long enough to facilitate an escape.

4. Experiment with how to increase the pressure against an opponent on the ground. How can you lower your center of gravity above the press without risking a loss of balance?

Note that the reason a properly applied joint lock works so well is because there is no "slack," making the pain in the joint severe and immediate. You will get instant compliance, and there is no opportunity for your opponent to fight back. The same is true for presses, with the added benefit that they don't require fine motor skills to apply. Pressing against the bony areas of your opponent's body, especially if he is in contact with the ground, makes him unable to move with the technique. When there is no "slack," the effect of the press is immediate, with little opportunity for your opponent to counter.

# Weapon Presses

The beauty (and danger) of a weapon is that it lacks sensitivity. When striking with your fist, you run the risk of injuring yourself in the process. This is because of *Newton's Third Law of Motion*, which states that for every action there is an equal and opposite reaction. The force on your fist and the target are equal and opposite. However, because a weapon has no sensitivity, it is obvious that your opponent will get hurt more than you. Although a weapon, such as a stick, can break from the force of a blow, it cannot feel the pain.

Another benefit is that a stick is generally harder and less flexible than your arm or hand. When there is little give, it is easier to focus the force over a smaller surface area. The drawback of training with a weapon is that you must go at a lighter and slower pace to allow your training partner to "tap out" before he is injured.

The bonier the target, the more painful the press is. When two hard surfaces make contact, and neither is flexible, the effect can be severe. Take a few minutes and start with the head of your body, work your way down, and identify any target that has a bone protruding. Some good targets for weapon presses are: eyebrows, bridge of nose, temples or sides of the skull, back of neck, jaw line, philtrum (below the nose), ears, windpipe (this can cause death), collar bones, ribs if you roll or knead the stick, hip bones, knuckles on fingers and hands, ulna bones on wrists, elbows, knees (both below and across), shin bones, ankle bones, bones in foot, and knuckles on toes.

The strongest way to hold the stick is horizontally with one hand at each end. This allows you to press the stick into the target in conjunction with a kneading motion. If your opponent moves or struggles to get away, he may actually intensify the pain. Keep your own center of gravity low, and rely on the entire weight of your body, if possible. Keep your arms slightly bent. If you press with straight arms, you are at a greater risk of losing balance if your opponent counters your move.

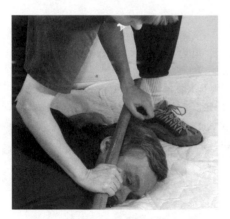

**Use a stick to intensify pressure against any bony areas of your opponent's body. Try to place as much body weight as possible directly above the press. The head is always a good target, since controlling the head helps you control the body. If possible, have your opponent facing away from you.**

You can also use the tip of the stick to press against a specific and small area of your opponent's body, or to press into soft tissue areas: side of the neck just below the jaw line, the soft spot above the collar bones, abdominal region below the ribcage, or solar plexus. Applying pressure with the tip instead of the length of the stick is a little more difficult, because you must be more precise with the target and can't use both hands in a kneading motion. However, the tip has the potential for more pounds of pressure per square inch, and can therefore dig deeply into the target. Note that although the study of pressure points is an exact science that we will not get into in this book, in general, it can be said that nerves emerge at any soft spot, indentation, or cavity on your opponent's body, making these effective pain compliance targets when using your fingers or the tip of the stick.

## How to Hold the Stick

If you have the opportunity to pick up a stick *after* being confronted by an assailant, his focus is likely to shift to the stick momentarily. This could give you a time advantage. When an unexpected weapon suddenly shows up, our perceptions of what's going to happen change, and we generally become more cautious. However, it may also increase your opponent's urge to get his attack under way. Either way, it will give you a brief window of opportunity, while his brain makes the connection between the weapon and the situation.

If your opponent is also wielding a weapon, be aware that you might get "hypnotized" by the weapon. You will be thinking about striking or blocking his hand or the weapon, more than you will be thinking about offense. If you have reach on your opponent with the stick, try striking his head or some other highly sensitive area, like the knee or wrist. Rather than focusing on disarming him, focus on incapacitating him.

Try a two-handed horizontal grip on the stick to block your opponent's strike, and drive the tip of the stick into his eyes or throat. Use body momentum to maintain contact with the target and continue driving forward and down, until your opponent goes to the ground. Be aware of his free hand, especially if you are positioned along his centerline. Whenever possible take up the superior position behind your opponent.

**Block an attack and drive the tip of the stick into a soft tissue area.**

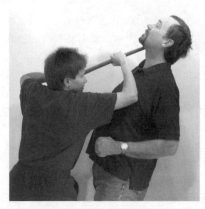

You can also block the strike to the outside of the arm, pinning your opponent's arm to his body. Use a two-handed horizontal grip moving forward while the stick is still in contact with his arm. If you lose contact, keep the stick close to your center of mass and rely on body momentum to apply a press across your opponent's throat. Because the press is applied above his center of gravity, it will unbalance him to the rear. Don't allow your momentum to stop. Think beyond blocking the attack. For the purpose of this book, your objective is always an unbalancing move.

**Block an attack, using a two-handed grip on the stick, and move forward with a press to your opponent's upper body or throat. Maintain contact with the target until your opponent goes down. Remember to direct the energy properly. Note also the proximity of your body to your opponent's, which allows you to use body momentum rather than arm strength alone.**

## Safety Tips

1. When practicing weapon presses to the neck, apply pressure slightly to the side of the windpipe, and not directly against it. Apply gentle pressure only.

2. With your partner's consent, increase pressure slowly to allow him to feel the realism of the technique. Release the pressure immediately when he taps out.

3. The pressure increases quickly when using the tip of the stick. Remember the no sensitivity principle – you are not able to tell how much pressure you apply through the stick. Exercise caution and listen to your partner when he tells you to stop.

# Stick Grabbing Exercise

The stick can be held in a variety of ways. Experiment with both hands palm down, and with one hand palm down and the other palm up. What benefits does each grip give you?

1. If you have to let go of the stick with one hand and use it as a striking weapon, which grip will best lend itself to this?

2. If you are under attack, and you have the opportunity to find an object in the environment that resembles a stick, it is likely "end up" in what is the most natural grip for you. Most people grip it palm down if picking it up with only one hand. Identify which grip is most natural for you, and practice striking with the stick from this grip.

3. Practice grabbing the other end of the stick with your free hand in what feels most natural for the situation. Can you use the stick as a press from this grip?

4. What will you do if your opponent tries to take the stick from you? If your opponent yanks the stick violently and you are still holding on, you may get yanked off balance, making it difficult to start an offensive technique against him. If you are unable to react in time to twist the stick from his grip, it may be better to let go of it and move into an empty hand unbalancing technique right away. Don't fight the opponent at his point of strength (his grip on the stick). However, be aware of that it *is* our natural reaction to do so. Experiment with a partner who is grabbing the stick while you are still holding onto it. Try to go with the motion of his attack and into a press or unbalancing technique.

**Your Mindset**

**If your mind-set is on countering force with force, you are not likely to succeed. Experiment with letting go of the stick and moving into an unbalancing technique.**

# Blocking and Striking with the Stick

It takes more force to block a strike thrown with intent than most untrained people think. Defense is not as simple as learning a few variations of blocks. Blocking a front kick with the palm of your hand, for example, is not likely to be effective, especially not when your opponent is wearing shoes. However, because a stick lacks sensitivity, and because it covers a relatively large area, it has the potential to be an effective blocking weapon. If your opponent throws a front kick, meet the momentum of his kick by dropping your body slightly forward and jamming the stick horizontally into his shinbone. Connect before his leg is fully extended to keep from taking the kick.

Make the block definite. Holding the stick with both hands and using the middle portion to block makes for a stronger block. But sometimes it is necessary to hold the stick with only one hand, perhaps if time is a factor, or if you need the greater distance the one handed grip affords you. A one handed grip takes more strength, because the lever arm (from your hand to the point of the block) is longer, so the torque on your hand is greater and could rip the stick from your grip.

After you have blocked, use the stick as an offensive weapon, immediately entering into a striking attack to your opponent's head or to other bony targets on his body. Rely on the first touch concept. As soon as the block is complete, it should trigger your follow-up strike. There should be no pause between block and strike. Remember, we are assuming that you are in a situation that is a threat to your life. Keep in mind the no sensitivity principle. When fighting bare fisted, you can usually feel how much damage you are doing. But since you can't feel anything through a weapon, it is easy to do a lot of damage fast. One single blow to a vital target may be fatal. You can also lunge forward into a press and unbalancing move after blocking.

**Your Mindset** **Strike with the intent of going through the target – one hard blow. Don't whack half-heartedly back and forth.**

If your opponent is wielding a knife, blocking the attack with your hand or arm is risky. A stick gives you more protection through its longer reach. It also gives you a psychological advantage. Use the stick to strike your opponent's arm from a distance, preferably the bones in his hand, knuckles, and wrist.

When striking with the stick, the greatest power at the tip is achieved by holding the stick as close to one end as possible. However, the longer the stick, the more force it takes to swing it, so a stick that is too long may seem impractical. The weight distribution as well as the distance to your target may differ, which becomes especially apparent if holding the stick at one end. It is easy to see a long stick as a long range weapon only. However, any technique that you can do with a short stick can be adapted to a long stick. A long stick has great short range capabilities as well, especially when used as a press. Understanding this enables you to use any length stick, or any object that resembles a stick, according to the same principles.

## Standing Immobilization Presses

For a press to work, it must preclude your opponent from moving with the pressure. It therefore makes little sense to press your opponent if he has the ability to step back. Using the ground as a stabilizer is effective but requires that your opponent is lying down. Standing presses can be applied using your own body as the stabilizer, and are especially effective if you use a stick to intensify the pressure.

Start by controlling your opponent's head. Hold the stick with both hands, placing it around his neck, so that his head is in the space between your arms. Pull your opponent toward you. Remember the bony areas of his anatomy. These are the ones that lend themselves best to presses, and therefore to pain compliance.

**Use your own body as a stabilizer when pressing toward you. Note how the opponent is off balance to the rear. If he grabs the stick, you still have a good chance of taking him down, as long as you don't allow his C.G. to shift forward again. Continue walking back while pressing your opponent to the ground.**

**Caution: Don't allow your own C.G. to shift to the rear with his body weight on top of you. Widen your base for balance.**

1. If approaching from the side, wrap the stick around your opponent's head and press against his jaw.

2. If approaching from the rear, wrap the stick around your opponent's head and press across his chin, windpipe, bridge of nose, or philtrum.

If your opponent's arm gets trapped along with his neck in the space between your arms, as might happen when he tries to keep the stick from contacting his neck, ignore it. As long as the stick contacts bony areas, it can be used for pain compliance. Pressing against your opponent's wrist or back of hand, for example, is effective when you are unable to make direct contact with his neck.

The standing immobilization press without a stick can be used as a rescue technique. Approach your opponent from the rear, using your forearm to press against his eye socket or across the bridge of his nose. This causes intense pain and splits his focus away from the attack. Clasp your hands together and place your forearm into the target. Make the grip and press definite. Don't leave any space between your body and the opponent. Pull his head into your body with your forearm. Continue stepping back until he goes down.

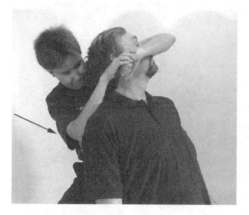

**Forearm press against the bridge of nose and cheekbone. Clasp your hand or wrist to tighten the grip. Note how the elbow is used against the opponent's back in conjunction with the push-pull principle as a second point of balance.**

# Figure Four Press

It has been said that, once applied, the figure four choke (sleeper hold) is nearly inescapable. However, if you are under great stress trying to apply it, your opponent may get out of it by pressing his chin down toward his chest or by hunching his shoulders. If the choke fails, you still have the option of a press from the figure four lock. As you feel your opponent's head slide down through your arms, use the figure four as a "jaw choke," applying pressure against the hinges of your opponent's jaw. This is extremely painful and gives your opponent the sensation that you are "spreading his teeth apart." Remember, all you have to do to tighten the technique is to hunch your shoulders.

**Figure four press against the jaw. This technique is identical to the figure four choke; only the target differs.**

You can also use the same technique against the philtrum, across the bridge of the nose, or across the temples and eyes. Above the eyebrows is usually less effective, as the head tapers off, making an escape easier.

# Tightening The Press

Many presses that utilize the stick around your opponent's neck or body can be tightened by placing the stick horizontally in the crooks of your arms, rather than holding each end in your hands. This also frees up your hands. For example, place the stick against the side of your opponent's neck from a position behind him, with the ends of the stick in the crooks of your arms. Place your free hands against the back of your opponent's head and push his head forward and into the stick. You are now pulling the stick toward you with the crooks of your arms and elbows, and pushing the opponent's head away from you with your hands, utilizing the push-pull principle. This intensifies the pressure through the use of opposing forces.

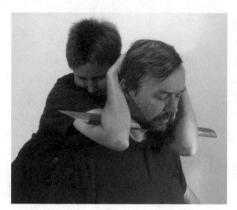

**Choking press with stick in the crooks of your arms. The hands push the head forward to tighten the press against the throat. Tuck your own chin down behind your shoulder to protect your face against your opponent's hands.**

**Caution:** It takes very little effort to tighten and increase the pressure in this type of technique. Be especially careful when working with the stick against your partner's throat.

Your next step is the unbalancing technique. If you are up against a stronger opponent, and he manages to get a hand up to the stick, it is possible that he can break your grip. The unbalancing move must therefore be a priority as soon as you have split your opponent's focus with the press. It is important to understand how a technique can fail, so that you don't continue struggling at the point of your opponent's strength. No technique works on everybody all of the time. When a technique fails, it will stun you, block your thought process, or make you repeat your mistake. Studying failure, and how to proceed after a failed technique, can therefore be a lifesaver.

Note that getting to the superior position behind your opponent may be tricky unless you can take him by surprise. If you approach your opponent from the front and place the stick around the back of his neck and pull toward you, he will end up with his face against your chest. What are his defensive capabilities from this position? Can he bite you? Can he knee you in the groin?

# Presses Against the Arms

Standing immobilization presses don't have to be executed against your opponent's head. If you see an opportunity to lock his arm against your body, you can execute a press against the inherent weakness of the elbow. A press to one of your opponent's arms, combined with forward momentum, can also be used to lock your opponent's other arm against his own body. Continue carrying your momentum forward, simultaneously stepping behind your opponent's foundation to unbalance him to the rear.

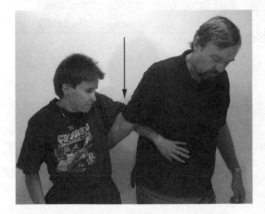

**This press utilizes your own body as a stabilizer, while your arm exerts pressure to the back of your opponent's elbow. A sudden twist in your hips can hyperextend the elbow and damage the ligaments. When your opponent reacts, continue with an unbalancing move.**

**Press one of your opponent's arms into his other arm, and use forward momentum to unbalance him to the rear. Note how the person executing the press remains close to the opponent. A leg immobilization technique might work well in conjunction with the press.**

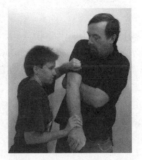

# Immobilization Presses from the Ground

The ground, in conjunction with other body parts, can be used as a barrier to immobilize your target. For example, if your opponent is on his stomach, use the stick in conjunction with a weaponless body part as a press to control him. Place your knee on his wrist or on the small bones in his hand, and the stick across his elbow. Lean forward to place your weight above the stick. Or place one knee on your opponent's wrist, the other on his elbow or shoulder, and the stick across the back of his neck. Hold the stick with both hands and exert downward pressure. If possible, turn your opponent's head away from you, so that he can't see what you are doing. This gives you additional psychological control.

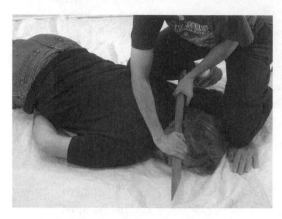

**Attacking two points simultaneously splits your opponent's focus and increases the effectiveness of the press. Note the knee on top of the hand, and how the opponent's other hand is trapped under his body.**

You don't need to have knowledge of complicated joint locks to be successful with presses. Think like this: How can I go against the natural movement of the joint? When your opponent is on his stomach on the ground, turn his arm with the elbow up and use a knee press to the back of and slightly above his elbow, simultaneously pulling up on his wrist. His arm is lying horizontally against the floor, with the force of the technique going against the natural bend of the elbow.

Do the same technique with his arm in the vertical position. Your opponent is on his stomach on the ground, and you are standing. Place your foot against the back of his shoulder to pin him to the ground. With his arm vertically straight, place his elbow against your leg, which acts as a barrier, and pull his arm against its natural movement. Regardless of your position, use whatever body part you can to stabilize the arm, so that any pressure against the joint results in severe pain or injury. Make sure the slack is taken out of the arm first.

**Standing foot press with control of the elbow. The elbow should be turned toward your leg. Exert pressure through opposing movements: push or pull the opponent's hand toward your leg, simultaneously pushing your knee against his elbow.**

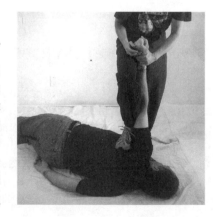

From a position on the ground, rest your opponent's arm against your shoulder and side of head and execute a knee press to his head. Place the stick behind your opponent's elbow and pull toward you, simultaneously leaning forward. If you roll the stick across his elbow while also applying determined pressure, the pain from the press is likely to be excruciating and will split your opponent's focus instantly.

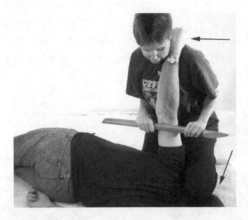

**Arm immobilization technique using the side of your head and a stick to the elbow. Note also the knee press to the opponent's head.**

Any lock becomes more effective when the opponent's body is kept from moving. Think in terms of how you can keep your opponent's joint from moving. How can you turn the joint so as to exert pressure against it?

Next, try the bent arm lock variation. Your opponent is on his stomach, and you pin his shoulder with your knee. Bend your opponent's arm behind his back, grab his wrist and pull it up toward his head along the centerline of his back. Do not allow his arm to make contact with his back, as this increases his flexibility and keeps the lock from having an immediate effect. Think of the move as going in two directions simultaneously: toward his head and up toward the ceiling. Because the shoulder is immobilized, he can't move with the technique.

**Shoulder press with bent arm lock. For greater effect, keep the opponent's arm from touching his back.**

# Body Elongation Presses

Most presses are thought to "compress" a part of your opponent's body. But a more unorthodox press involves elongating your opponent's body instead by pushing his head away from his feet, placing stress on the neck and spine. For example, you are on the ground with your opponent, and when you try to get back to your feet, he trips you by trapping your legs with his. You fall with your head away from his and your feet toward his head. If your opponent has one of your legs locked with his, rather than trying to free it and get to your feet, use it as a stabilizing point and press with your free foot against his chin to elongate his body.

**Push with your free foot against your opponent's chin, simultaneously pulling his arm toward you. This press will elongate his neck.**

The body elongation press also works from a kneeling position with your opponent on his side. Place a knee press into his ribs, keep control of his arm, and place your free hand under his chin and pull back until his neck and body are arched.

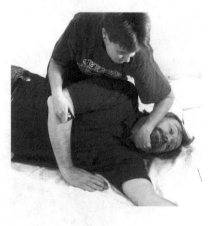

**Variation of body elongation press. Stabilize the body by pushing your knee into your opponent's back.**

A third option against a sitting or standing opponent: stabilize his shoulders and tilt or twist his head to the end of its range of motion. You have now accomplished a sideways neck elongation. Use the push-pull principle with your hands, while the rest of your body or some outside barrier stabilizes your opponent's shoulders.

## Multiple Simultaneous Presses

Whenever you have the option, rely on more than one press at a time. For example, from a position on the ground, press the stick into the side of your opponent's neck, and your knee into his lower rib cage. Control at two points is more effective than at one point, as long as it allows you full focus on the controlling technique. Don't spread your two points so far apart that pressure, or pounds per square inch, is sacrificed. The more your weight is directly above the target, the greater the pounds per square inch. Sometimes this requires a more upright stance, which may lessen your stability. It is important to keep your arms bent and use the full weight of your body when pressing.

**Think about this**

**If your opponent grabs your arm, your focus is likely to split from the press to defense. This is your first sign of weakness, and may turn the fight to your opponent's advantage.**

Pressing against the side of our opponent's neck can stop the blood flow to the brain and cause unconsciousness. This is true even if you only have access to one side of his neck. If your opponent is lying on his back with you straddling him, use both your knees to press against his lower ribs and the stick to press against his throat, neck, or face. Be careful not to raise your center of gravity by "standing" on your knees.

**Reminder**

**A press with an insensitive stick to your opponent's windpipe can cause death. Unless there is a threat to your life, be selective with the techniques you use.**

# Thumb and Finger Presses

If your opponent is straddling you, press your thumbs into the soft areas under his chin to the sides of the windpipe. If the technique is done with intent, you are likely to get an immediate reaction with your opponent withdrawing his head. An immediate follow-up with an unbalancing move, while his center of gravity is high, can help you reverse positions. When you have reversed positions, use the ground to stabilize your opponent's body and follow with a knee press to his head.

A thumb press to the arteries on the sides of the neck is an effective press if done correctly. You must keep your hands from moving in order to gain maximum and quick pressure. Use your opponent's collar as a stabilizer. Many people are under the impression that a collar choke uses the collar to choke the opponent, and so question its effectiveness, especially if the shirt he is wearing is elastic. But when executing the thumb press, the collar does not provide the choke; it merely acts to stabilize your hands. If the shirt is elastic, grab the collar closer to the back of the neck to eliminate the slack.

With your elbows facing out, and the backs of your hands toward each other, grip the insides of your opponent's collar with both hands. Your fingers will be inside the shirt with your thumbs pressing against your opponent's carotid arteries. Your arms should be bent. Straighten your arms and observe how your thumbs move together quickly. This puts tremendous pressure on the arteries in your opponent's neck in a very short time.

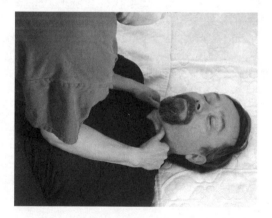

**Thumb press collar choke. As long as you have a steady grip on your opponent's collar, the pressure increases as a result of straightening your arms. If the collar is flimsy, reach around to the back of the neck to eliminate the slack.**

Note that if you don't use the collar as a stabilizer, your hands will move away from each other when you straighten your arms, and the pressure against the arteries will not be sufficient to choke your opponent.

If your opponent reaches out to grab you around the neck, lapels, or shoulders, and you don't have the reach to execute a palm and unbalancing move to his chin, you can spear two crossed fingers into his throat (the soft spot below the Adam's apple). Continue driving forward and down. Note that this is not a poke, but a soft tissue press with continuous downward motion, and demonstrates the strength and effectiveness of a finger when used against an appropriate target.

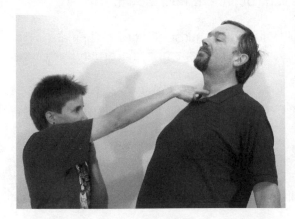

**Finger press to the throat. Keep fingers in contact with the target until you have unbalanced your opponent. The press must be done with intent and forward momentum to keep your opponent from grabbing your arm and negating the press.**

# Common Mistakes

### 1. Failing to apply pressure with intent.

Don't let up when your opponent stops struggling. Be prepared to intensify the pressure by lowering your body weight or applying a kneading motion.

### 2. Stalling your attack once your opponent goes down.

A press may be difficult to apply when in the midst of a grappling match. Try to apply the press the moment your opponent hits the ground after an unbalancing move.

### 3. Losing awareness of your own stability.

Be careful not to be in a position where your own foundation is unstable, as when trying to use a heel press against your opponent from a standing position.

### 4. Discounting the use of the tip of the stick.

We have talked a lot about how to apply presses holding the stick with both hands, but don't discount the use of the tip of the stick. The tip allows you to focus the power over a smaller area.

### 5. Failing to use any available weapon as an equalizer.

Taking a full power kick from an assailant wearing shoes can have a damaging outcome. Using a weapon, such as a stick, to block, acts as an equalizer and decreases the risk of getting hurt.

### 6. Presenting your opponent with an opportunity to disarm you.

Any time you extend a weapon toward your opponent, you also give him the opportunity to disarm you. Keep the weapon close to your body and move forward with explosiveness and intent, relying on body momentum.

# 8

# Stick Leverage
# Unbalancing Moves

Many people think of a stick as a striking weapon but, as we have already begun to learn, it is also a great leverage and pressout weapon. A stick can help you create *torque*, or a mechanical advantage to further help you manipulate your opponent's position, eliminating the need for a lot of strength. The insensitivity of the stick makes it easy to apply pressure intense enough to make your opponent comply. The stick can therefore be used as a press and unbalancing weapon with greater efficiency than your hand, arm, or leg.

A stick can also be used to extend the length of your arms. If you have short arms, it may be difficult to reach around a much bigger opponent in an unbalancing move and get a good grip. The stick can be used to extend your reach by grabbing the stick with one hand at each end and wrapping your arms and the stick around your opponent's body. When using the stick this way, do not leave a gap between the stick and your opponent's body. Hold the stick so that it is tight against the area you wish to control. A gap gives your opponent an opportunity to escape, and may also cost you time, because the technique won't be effective until the "slack" has been eliminated. Tighten the gap by sliding your hands closer together on the stick.

## Lesson Objectives

At the end of this lesson, you should understand:

1. How to use momentum to push your opponent off balance with the stick
2. How to use two points of balance with the stick
3. Why it is important to eliminate the slack
4. How to increase the effectiveness of rear takedowns
5. How to increase the effectiveness of forward takedowns

# Pushing Unbalancing Moves with the Stick

The stick can be used in a simple body push attack relying on your forward momentum. Hold the stick horizontally with one hand at each end. Keep the stick close to your body and use body momentum to push your opponent back or down.

Don't extend your arms prior to the attack, as this presents your opponent with the opportunity to grab the stick. Also, you cannot generate as much momentum if pushing with your arms alone. Because of the greater mass of your body, the push should originate in your legs, as if trying to walk through your opponent with the intent of replacing his body's position with your own. Your power is focused in the center of your body, so all attacks that involve pushing or balance manipulation should be kept close to the center. This is contrary to using the stick for striking, where distance may be to your advantage.

If your opponent grabs one end of the stick and tries to take it from you, it is imperative that you react immediately to avoid getting into a wrestling match with him. The moment he grabs the stick, use a small circular motion of the tip to twist the stick from his grip. This, too, involves the push-pull principle. Increase leverage by using both hands. The farther apart your hands are on the stick, the easier it is to start a torque, or rotation. This is because the lever arm is longer so less force, or muscular effort, is needed.

**Use torque to twist the stick from your opponent's grip. For maximum effect, keep wide separation between your hands.**

# Two Points of Balance

When working with the stick, the principle of two points of balance applies. If you rely on a natural bend in your opponent's body, you can increase the effectiveness of the takedown. The small of the back is such a point. By putting pressure against the small of the back, you bring your opponent's hips forward, moving his upper body to the rear. You may have seen this technique with the practitioner applying a front bear hug around the waist of his adversary. But if you are of small stature, and your opponent has a strong back or a large upper body, it may be difficult to reach around him and exert enough pressure to succeed with the technique. The stick extends your reach and increases the intensity of the attack.

**Bear hug unbalancing move, using a natural bend in the body. The technique should be forceful with a simultaneous push with your shoulder against your opponent's upper body.**

Take this a step further by manipulating your opponent's foundation, simultaneously relying on momentum to steal his balance. If you can hook one of your legs around his leg, and simultaneously push forward against his upper body, you can shift the C.G. easier than if you rely on the small of his back alone. Be aware of your opponent's free hands so that he doesn't use them against you. Just as with any unbalancing move, it must be swift and determined to be successful.

**Reminder**

**If you give your opponent the opportunity, he will not only try to counter the technique, he will also negate it by rounding his back or by taking a step to the rear, creating a gap between you.**

Regardless of which type of unbalancing move you use, always work along the centerline of your body. For this particular technique, this means bringing your elbows in toward your centerline. Aside from giving you better strength and control, this also tightens the space between your arms, making the technique more definite.

The centerline principle applies when using the stick to push against your opponent's body as well. If you hold the stick at each end, and your elbows are pointing to your sides, it is difficult to place your entire weight behind the technique, and your arms may collapse under the resistant force of your opponent's body. Although I don't recommend keeping the arms straight, I do recommend bringing your elbows in toward the center of your body, if possible.

## Eliminating the Slack

In all the takedowns you practice, focus on taking the slack out of the technique. Not only does this give you more control, it also gives you a psychological advantage. Even if the pressure isn't so intense that your opponent is helpless, the fact that the hold is tight will make him *feel* so. This is why it is important that all techniques are done with intent. Every move must be felt and kept close to your own center of mass. For example:

1. In a single leg takedown, shoot at your opponent's legs and wrap the stick around his calf, pulling his foot toward you. Keep the space between your body and your opponent's leg as tight as possible. After contacting your opponent's calf, roll the stick down to his Achilles tendon and pull his foot toward you, simultaneously driving forward with your shoulder above his knee. Hold the stick with both hands and use your shoulder against your opponent's thigh as your second point of balance.

2. In a head takedown, push the stick horizontally under your opponent's chin to shift his weight to the rear. Your arms should be bent with your elbows "sucked in" toward your centerline, making the gap between your body and the technique as tight as possible. Your second point of balance is your hip, with your leg (behind your opponent's leg) acting as a barrier to stabilize your opponent's foundation.

3. When wrapping the stick around your opponent's neck, tighten the grip by placing the stick in the crooks of your arms instead of holding it with your hands. Your hands are now palm up rather than palm down. This gives you great leverage, and all you have to do to intensify pressure is to bend your arms and bring your hands toward you as if doing a bicep curl.

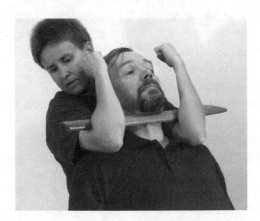

Take the slack out by placing the stick in the crooks of your arms. Note how the opponent's weight is to the rear.

**Caution:** Use extreme care when practicing with a stick against your opponent's throat. For practice purposes, place the stick slightly to one side of the neck, rather than directly against the windpipe.

The slack can be taken out of the technique either by moving your body toward your opponent's body, or by pulling your opponent toward you. Which one you use depends on whether you are taking your opponent down toward you or away from you. If your arms are bent, there is automatically less slack, because it places you closer to your opponent. Your mind-set should be on closeness and not on distance. Trying to keep your opponent away while simultaneously trying to unbalance him is counterproductive, because you can't rely on the full strength of your body.

The stick is easier to get a good grip on than is your opponent's arm, leg, or neck, and taking the slack out allows you to control a struggling opponent better. A stick that is used as an extension of your arm, that has no sensitivity, and that affords you a good grip with more leverage, makes your techniques easier to execute.

## Rear Takedown with the Stick

When approaching a standing opponent from behind with the intent of taking him down to the rear, the faster you walk back after placing the stick around his neck, the less likely he is to step with the technique to retain balance. His first thought will be on the stick and his neck. Take wide steps, keeping your own balance. Once your opponent's legs are lagging behind his upper body C.G., dropping him to the ground is easy.

When your opponent goes down, kneel down with him, continuing the pressure against his throat, or let go and run as he begins to fall. If you go down with your opponent, you can also place one of your knees on the stick to help intensify the pressure. However, remember that to every action there is an equal and opposite reaction. If you press with your knee into the stick (which presses against your opponent's throat or face), the pressure you exert on the stick is equal and opposite that exerted on your knee. If you are wearing heavy pants that give you some protection, this might be a good technique.

Sometimes it is easier to reach around your opponent's head (from a position behind him) and grab his chin with one hand and tilt his head back first, *then* place the stick against one side of his neck and grab it with the other hand. This allows you to steal your opponent's balance before his mind is on the stick, making him less likely to fight for control of the stick.

## Forward Takedown with the Stick

It is more difficult to unbalance an opponent forward than to the rear. This is because the body is naturally quite flexible to the front. We have discussed how an object in the environment can be used to stabilize your opponent's foundation, so that he can't take a step for balance. If you don't have access to such a barrier, the stick allows you to increase the effectiveness of a forward unbalancing move. For example, if your opponent is coming toward you with his head low in a tackle, side-step the attack and shove the stick horizontally against the back of his neck, pressing down hard on his neck until he goes down. Use your whole body weight, so that you are almost lying on top of your opponent. It is not necessary to go all the way to the ground with your opponent, but the technique must be definite to be effective. Remember that if you allow a gap to form between the target and the stick before you have shifted your opponent's C.G., it affords him the possibility to escape.

If you can intensify your opponent's motion in the direction he is already going, you will save energy and make the takedown more dynamic. If your opponent approaches you in a tackle with his head low, meeting power with power and trying to straighten his body so you can take him down to the rear, takes a greater effort than if you capitalize on the motion he has already started. What makes this different from a simple hair pull is that the stick gives you more control across the whole back of your opponent's neck, which makes it a difficult technique to escape. The position of your hands at both ends of the stick gives you great strength, in conjunction with your body weight, in the downward direction. Once your body weight is above your opponent, a downward *push*, rather than a downward *pull* allows you to take full advantage of it.

A forward takedown from a position behind your opponent, as when coming to the aid of another person, can be quite violent if you manipulate your opponent's foundation rather than his upper body. Stabilize the base and move your opponent's upper body center of gravity forward by "pulling his feet out from under him." However, this technique is difficult if your opponent is big and weighs a lot, and especially if he is in a stance with one foot forward for stability. The stick can increase your strength and effectiveness. Wrap it around your opponent's legs, slightly below his kneecaps, to keep him from bending his legs. The stick gives you leverage and splits your opponent's focus through pain. Pull the stick toward you, using both hands equally, and drive your upper body into the upper part of the back of your opponent's legs. Because your opponent can't bend his legs, he will hit the ground hard, and will try to steady himself with his hands. If he is holding a weapon, he may lose it at this time.

**Stabilize your opponent's foundation with the stick, and push his upper body center of gravity forward.**

Keeping the stick tight is important, as it keeps the opponent from turning his body prior to impacting the ground. The impact will seem more violent if he falls on his face rather than on his side.

# Common Mistakes

### 1. Attempting to push your opponent away.

Unbalancing techniques require close proximity to your opponent. This can be repulsive when you are trying to get away rather than staying to fight. But it is difficult to use the full weight of your body if the technique is not executed close to your own center of mass. Keep your arms bent and take the slack out of the technique.

### 2. Neglecting the many uses of the stick.

The stick is not exclusively a striking or blocking weapon, nor is it exclusively a leverage weapon. Understand the *no sensitivity principle* and how it increases your control.

### 3. Failing to use a mechanical advantage to disarm your opponent.

When you have access to a weapon, your opponent is likely to become fixated on the weapon and on trying to take it from you. Use torque to wrestle the stick from a stronger opponent.

# 9 | Rearward Throws

Now that we have looked at the concepts of balance manipulation in takedowns from standing and on the ground, we will learn how to utilize these same principles of center of gravity, momentum, and torque to throw an adversary.

A throw is generally more violent than a takedown, and therefore has a potentially higher success rate. But because of resistance from the opposing party and difficulty to attain correct positioning, throws don't always work. A smaller person cannot simply pick up somebody who is big and heavy and threatening and throw him to the ground. A smaller person must rely on scientific principles rather than on strength.

Depending on how the situation unfolds, and as long as you understand that both throws and takedowns utilize the same principles of motion, you can use either a throw or a takedown, with the main difference being positioning. While a takedown permits some space between you and your opponent, most throws require that you position hip to hip with your opponent (touching). In addition, throws utilize a tight circular motion over the top of your hip or body, while takedowns utilize a larger circle around your body. There are many ways to throw an adversary, but they all rely on just a few scientific principles, with *torque* (leverage) being the primary principle of throwing.

When threatened by an adversary, your initial intent may be to start with a takedown. But when your opponent resists or tries to counter, you may feel a need to get him on the ground as quickly as possible. If you see an opportunity to transition from the takedown to a throw, the technique is likely to be more dynamic and slam your opponent harder against the ground. Because takedowns and throws are so similar, transitioning from a takedown to a throw is relatively easy and a good opportunity should the takedown fail. The same is true in reverse. If you attempt to throw your adversary, and your balance point isn't quite right, you may still be able to pull off the takedown variation.

The most common throws are hip throws, where you utilize your hip as the balance point. Distance is important. There is only one distance that is optimal, but a lot of takedowns and throws "end up" at other distances as well. The optimal distance for a throw is hip to hip with your opponent, where you place your hip in the center of his body before applying downward leverage. If your hip is slightly too deep, you will end up carrying a lot of your opponent's weight, which requires more strength and effort. If your hip is slightly too much to the side, the throw will become more circular around your body, and lack the dynamics inherent to a correctly executed throw. Initially, reverse hip throws should be practiced facing the exact opposite direction of your opponent. This allows you to "lead" through body rotation. If you are facing perpendicular to your opponent, you run the risk of the motion exhausting itself halfway through the technique.

Many throws also utilize a controlling technique against the head or neck. As already discussed, the reason this is so effective is because the neck is an inherent weakness of our anatomy, and when the neck is controlled, the body must follow.

## Lesson Objectives

At the end of this lesson, you should be familiar with the following throws:

1. Reverse throw from figure four arm lock
2. Reverse throw from double hand neck manipulation
3. Reverse throw from cross wrist grab
4. Reverse throw using the body as leverage
5. Reverse throw from double hand shoulder grab
6. Reverse throw from wrist lock

## Center of Gravity and Momentum in Throws

When executing a throw, strive to make your and your opponent's center of gravity one and the same. Think of your opponent's body as part of you own. Once you achieve the same center of gravity, it is no more difficult manipulating your opponent's body than it is your own. Joining centers requires that there is no gap between your bodies. Nor should your opponent be allowed to slide down your hip, or over your upper back or shoulders. His weight must be centered on your own balance point. If it falls above it, you have a top heavy load; if it falls below it, you have to struggle with lifting his weight. Your ability to combine centers of gravity is what makes a correctly executed throw easy for a lighter weight person against a heavier opponent. Balancing a weight, even if it is a heavy weight, is easy when you find the balance point. When starting the throw, don't think in terms of "lifting" your opponent onto your hip or back. Rather, think in terms of placing your center of gravity in the same spot as his, and then manipulating his body the way you would your own.

Continue thinking of your and your opponent's bodies as one and the same, until you need to let go and allow him to fall. This requires that you move together as one entity. Although you are the one leading the motion, don't move your body mass faster than your opponent's, as this requires you to expend energy by pulling him with you. On the other hand, if you move your body mass slower than your opponent's, you may lose balance due to the inertia of your opponent's momentum. This gives you the feeling that you are carrying his weight.

**When throwing, don't step and pull. Use your center of gravity to lead in the throw, synchronizing your momentum with your opponent's.**

**Think about this**

As already discussed, any defensive move has a higher success rate if your opponent is slightly unbalanced before you attempt the rest of the technique. It is possible to throw your opponent over your hip by raising both his feet off the ground simultaneously. But if you can unbalance him to one leg prior to throwing, his base is narrower, and shifting the center of gravity is easier. You can also unbalance your opponent by using forward momentum, for example, by stepping in with a forearm across his chest, a palm strike to his chin, or any other technique that causes his weight to shift to the rear. Stealing balance prior to throwing is especially important when your positions are equally superior, as is the case with the reverse hip throw.

**Use your momentum in combination with a leverage technique to move into your opponent's centerline and displace his center of gravity with your own.**

**Think about this**

## Learning to Fall

Since somebody will experience a violent fall every time a throw is practiced, it is essential that you and your practice partner learn how to properly absorb the shock of a fall. Most throws can initially be practiced from a kneeling position, until you get used to taking the fall. The shock is absorbed by:

1. Rounding your back and rolling with the technique, absorbing the shock sequentially over a large part of your body.

2. Spreading your weight as wide as possible, lessening the force per square inch. Don't allow your head to touch the ground. Tuck your chin down toward your chest.

A detailed analysis of falling will not be discussed in this book. Refer to the safety box in the introduction for additional tips on falling.

## Reverse Throw from Figure Four Arm Lock

Use this throw any time you see an opportunity to apply a figure four lock on your opponent's arm. For example:

1. When an assailant approaches you from the front and grabs you around the neck with one or both hands.

2. When an assailant is wielding a weapon, utilizing a downward swing.

Before we proceed with the throw, let's look at the mechanics of the figure four arm lock. Although this is a controlling technique against the joints, it is still considered gross motor skills, as it utilizes the large joint of the elbow (which is relatively easy to intercept) to lock out the shoulder.

**Have your partner raise his arm above his head as if to strike you with a downward motion. Block the technique with your forearm, using the arm that is on the opposite side (across) from your opponent's arm.**

**Cup your opponent's wrist or forearm with one hand, and bring your other hand around his arm and cup it on top of your own wrist.**

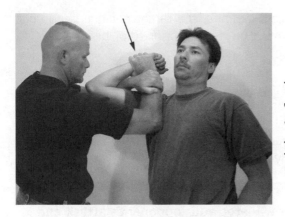

**The technique is called a "figure four" because of the 4 shape of your arms.**

If your opponent grabs you around the neck, the threat is not quite as high as if he swings at you with a weapon or his bare fist. When he grabs you, initiate the technique by "peeling" his hand off and bending his arm back into the figure four hold. How do you peel his hand off? The easiest way is by grabbing his little finger and twisting it hard against its natural movement.

**Peel your opponent's hand off your neck, and fold his arm back into the figure four.**

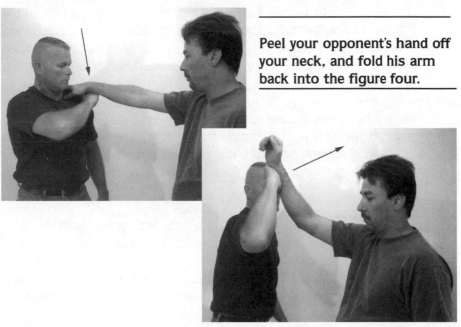

Remember, if it becomes a struggle, you don't want to stay with the technique. Your mind-set should be to react immediately upon being grabbed and, if possible, slightly before the grab has manifested itself. Don't forget the availability of your other weapons. Whenever a struggle ensues, use a softening technique. Any move that gets your opponent's upper body to the rear also has a tendency to lessen his grip. Try a palm strike to his jaw the moment he grabs you.

If your opponent is wielding a club or knife, the threat is higher, and your timing must be better. The arm must be stopped prior to or before reaching the apex of its downward motion.

- When you have achieved a figure four on the arm, step behind your opponent with the foot that is closest to his body. You are now hip to hip, facing opposite directions, with your position superior because of the figure four hold and the balance manipulation of your opponent's upper body to the rear.

**Reminder** **The figure four will stop your opponent's attack and give you controlling force, but it must be applied with intent to work.**

- Using the weight of your body, press your forearm or elbow against your opponent's shoulder without letting up on the figure four. This will continue to unbalance him to the rear. There should be no gap between your bodies. Push your hip into your opponent, with the intent of replacing his center of gravity with your own. Because you have stepped behind your opponent's foundation, pushing your hip into his will move your upper body forward in preparation for the throw.

- Throw your opponent diagonally backward over your hip by pivoting your body in a tight and quick downward spiral. If your opponent is at your right hip, think in terms of throwing him to the outside of your left foot. Your centers of gravity will join, making the throw seem effortless.

- Your opponent will land on his side or back by your feet. If choosing to continue control on the ground, use the figure four to turn your opponent to his stomach, and drop one knee into his ribs or onto the side of his head. This allows you to free your hands to take the weapon from him or apply a different control hold. Again, the knee press must be done with intent.

## Points to Consider

1. In any technique, your greatest strength is always along your centerline. When throwing the opponent using the figure four, bring your elbows in toward your center. This makes the hold stronger and eliminates a struggle against your own rotational inertia.

2. If using the takedown variation, the technique is identical, except that you are not stepping behind your opponent. Rather, sweep your leg in a large circle. The takedown variation allows some space between your bodies, resulting in a somewhat gentler fall.

**Reminder** **Rotational inertia = resistance to change in motion in an object that is rotating. The more centered the technique is about its rotational axis, the more energy conserving it is.**

Note that in a circular takedown (not throw), your and your opponent's centers of gravity are *not* one and the same. Because your opponent's body is farther from your C.G. than your body is (which is centered around it), he moves with a faster linear speed throughout the circle, which has a tendency to throw him off balance to the outside of the rotation. This makes it difficult for him to brace against the takedown, or to counter-attack effectively. However, the throw variation is more violent in the sense that it is quicker from start to finish, and your opponent will hit the ground harder.

## Reverse Throw from Double Hand Neck Manipulation

Use this throw any time you have the opportunity to establish the centerline (get your hands in between your opponent's hands). For example:

1. When your opponent approaches you from the front and reaches out to grab you around the neck with one or both hands.

2. When your opponent swings at you wildly in a "bar brawling" style.

3. When your opponent pushes your upper body with one or both hands.

4. When you initiate the technique, closing distance on an unsuspecting adversary.

If your opponent grabs you around the neck, place both your hands between his arms, or place one hand between his arms and the other around the outside of his arm. The hand that goes between the arms should grab the chin, and the other hand should grab the back of the head. Can you see how this is similar to the neck takedowns we have worked in previous chapters?

**Establish the centerline, and place one hand on his chin and the other on the back of his head. This gives you two points of balance. Note how distance is closed simultaneously to allow you to work around your center of gravity.**

**Reminder**

**Use the concept of *first touch*. Don't wait until your opponent has tightened his grip. React at the initiation of his move. This requires alertness to the potential dangers of the situation.**

If your opponent swings at you wildly, protect yourself by tucking your chin down and covering your head with your arms. At the moment of first touch (when you feel his blow land on your blocking arm), immediately move in and grab his chin with one hand and the back of his head with the other. The moment you block his punch, he will have to reset his body's balance before being able to throw an additional punch with the same hand. This is your window of opportunity.

Note that our natural reaction when somebody swings at us is to try to move back and out of harm's way. This is fine if you see the attack coming from a distance. But we often forget that sometimes safety is in closeness rather than in distance, and takedowns and throws are impossible to execute from a distance. Much of self-defense, as discussed in this book, is therefore about learning how to control your emotions and stay at close range, or even taking the initiative to close the gap on your opponent. A strike should be avoided if possible but, if moving to the rear, you must be aware of the additional time needed to reset your body's balance and execute your gap closure.

If your opponent pushes you, the technique is identical to if he reaches out to grab you. However, because a push is likely to knock you back or slightly off balance to the rear, your body must first correct itself by resetting your center of gravity. Your window of opportunity is right before your opponent attempts to push a second time. A push may be the first sign of an escalation of a verbal confrontation.

If you decide to take the offensive and initiate the technique, as might be the case when you try to de-escalate a situation or come to the rescue of another person, or when you have determined that the encounter has gone beyond trying to "talk your way out of it," you must close distance quickly and preferably use some sort of set-up or distracting technique first. For example, push off with your rear foot to gain momentum, and throw a front kick with your lead leg. Whether the kick lands or not is irrelevant, as long as it solicits the intended reaction of distracting your opponent and stalling his advance. Remember that once you start your forward momentum, do not stop until your opponent is lying harmless on the ground. When you have closed distance, grab your opponent's chin with one hand, and the back of his head with your other hand. Proceed as follows:

**When your opponent begins to lose balance, he will most likely try to steady himself by grabbing your neck or arm. As long as your balance is centered, and his is not, this should not cause you any problems when executing the throw. The shock from the impact with the ground should loosen his grip.**

- Step behind your opponent with the foot that is on the same side as the hand that is grabbing his chin. If you grab your opponent's chin with your right hand, your right foot is stepping behind your opponent's leg. You are now hip to hip with your opponent, facing opposite directions, with your position superior because of your control of his head. The back of your leg should make contact with the back of your opponent's leg, and you should already have started to take his balance to the rear.

- Continue tilting your opponent's head back by pushing up and back on his chin. This is the initial unbalancing move, which should be done forcefully prior to the throw. In fact, if for some reason you decide to abandon the throw, your opponent's center of gravity should have been shifted to the rear far enough to make him fall when you let go of him.

- As soon as you have taken your opponent's balance, turn his head to the side (toward your centerline), and throw him backward over your hip by pivoting your body in a tight downward spiral. Use the two points of balance on his head, with your hip as the center of rotation for the throw.

- Your opponent will land on his side or back close to your feet. You can now drop your knee straight down onto his head to pin it to the ground and proceed with another immobilization or controlling technique, if deemed necessary.

## Points to Consider

1. When your opponent starts to lose balance, he is likely to try to grab your clothing, neck, or arms in an attempt to steady himself. Don't release the grip on your opponent's head before he touches the ground. An early release may give him the opportunity to pull you down with him, which might hinder your escape or your ability to follow with a press to his head.

2. If using the takedown variation, the technique is identical, except that you are not stepping behind your opponent. Rather, sweep your leg (the one on the same side as the hand that grabs the back of your opponent's head) in a large circle, simultaneously pivoting your body in a downward spiral.

3. If the throw fails and you need to revert to the takedown variation, it is important to continue lowering your center of gravity smoothly throughout the unbalancing move. Our first reaction to a failed technique is to stall the momentum and try again, but by then you will have lost your window of opportunity.

# Reverse Throw from Cross Wrist Grab

Use this throw any time you have the opportunity to grab your opponent's wrist in a cross wrist grab. For example:

1. When your opponent grabs, or reaches out to grab, you.

2. After blocking or parrying a strike.

3. As an offensive move, where you initiate by grabbing first.

If your opponent reaches out to grab you, intercept his arm in a cross wrist grab. If he reaches for you with his right hand, use your right hand to grab his wrist. Again, this requires awareness of the situation. Most people will reach and close distance simultaneously. When your opponent starts to step toward you, it is likely that he will also begin extending his arm. This gives you a pre-warning and time to react. The technique can be used regardless of whether you grab your opponent's wrist or he grabs your wrist, and regardless of whether he grabs high (shoulder, neck) or low (belt).

**Think about this**

**An opponent who keeps his arms tight to his body and uses body momentum to close distance, instead of reaching, is more difficult to intercept.**

When you have intercepted your opponent's arm, pull it toward you and diagonally across your body to unbalance him in preparation for the throw. By pulling diagonally, you also use the strength of your centerline, which is one of the benefits of a cross wrist grab instead of a same side grab. Because the grip starts from the opposite side, you are pulling toward the center of your body, where your concerted balance and strength are.

**The cross wrist grab gives you control along your centerline.**

**The same side grab makes it more difficult to pull toward your centerline.**

The same principle can be applied after blocking or parrying a punch. When the block is complete, slide your hand down to your opponent's wrist and pull his arm toward you and diagonally across your body. Think of it as blocking and hooking your opponent's arm. You don't want to give him the opportunity to withdraw his arm again.

Note that it is not realistic to think that you have the speed and precision to catch and grab a strike that is thrown at you at full speed. However, blocking a strike is not that difficult. When attempting to grab, you should therefore block first. This will stall your opponent's momentum and freeze him for a fraction of a second, allowing you to hook and grab his wrist with the same hand that did the blocking. Blocking also gives you a sense of your opponent's rhythm. This is especially important if he is wielding a knife. Don't attempt to grab his knife wielding hand in mid-air and disarm him. Instead block, parry, or slap his arm to get a feel for his rhythm and stall his momentum, and then make a small circle around his wrist and grab.

**Think about this**

**Sometimes it is easier to grab *after* you have established contact with your opponent's arm. Your first thought should therefore be on blocking and not on grabbing.**

If blocking to the inside of your opponent's forearm with an inward block, use the same hand that is blocking to execute the cross wrist grab. If blocking to the outside of your opponent's arm, use the hand that is *not* blocking to execute the cross wrist grab. Don't think about it too much. Use what comes natural, and think in terms of concepts: *hook the arm and pull across your body.*

If you are the one initiating the technique, your initial move and distance closure must be quick. You must also have the mind-set to take the technique to conclusion. Try to set up your opponent with a fake. When he reacts, immediately close distance and grab his wrist in a cross wrist grab. Pull his arm toward you and diagonally across your body. Proceed as follows:

- When you have grabbed your adversary in the cross wrist grab and pulled him forward to unbalance him, he will be turned slightly sideways. This places you in the superior position behind his back.

- Grab your opponent's chin with your free hand. For this particular throw, don't reach around the back of his head. Your forearm will be in front of your face, with your thumb pointing toward the floor (see picture sequence below).

**The takedown variation is shown here. If this were a throw, you would be closing distance until you were hip to hip with your adversary, which would require that you let go of his arm once you had unbalanced him.**

- Step behind your opponent with the foot that is closest to the wrist grab, simultaneously letting go of his arm and sliding that hand up to his chin. You are now hip to hip, facing opposite directions, with your position superior because of your control of his head. Note that a hand change is needed. You must release your opponent's wrist in order to gain the mobility needed to execute the throw. This is not necessarily true for the takedown variation shown above. It is therefore imperative that you have taken your opponent's balance first, so that he doesn't use his free hand against you. The primary purpose of the cross wrist grab is to pull your opponent off balance, freeze him, and place him in an inferior position.

**This technique *can* be done reaching around the back of the head. When under stress, the technique will end up the way it ends up. You must then make the best of it.**

- Tilt your opponent's head back and to the side by pushing on his jaw. Throw him backward over your hip by pivoting your body in a downward spiral.

- Your opponent will land on his side or back. You can now release and run, or drop your knee onto his head and continue with another controlling technique.

## Points to Consider

1. Allowing the arm that controls the head to straighten will cause the technique to "exhaust itself," resulting in a throw that is too wide, allowing your opponent to step with the technique and regain balance. It will also result in too much *rotational inertia*, because the majority of the weight is away from the axis of rotation.

2. The grip on your opponent's wrist and head must be definite (done with intent). Even if your hands are small, or if the grip isn't strong enough to keep your opponent from breaking it, a definite grip gives you a psychological advantage.

3. If using the takedown variation, the technique is identical, except that you are using a wider sweeping motion with your leg. When starting the circular takedown, keep your opponent as close to your center as possible. Pull your opponent close through the cross wrist grab, keeping a slight bend in the elbow of your controlling arm.

## Faking Exercise

The purpose of a fake is to solicit a reaction, split your opponent's mind and body focus, and buy time to execute your distance closure. A fake must therefore look realistic. However, in a tense situation, any sudden move can solicit a reaction in your opponent. The problem is that if it isn't the reaction you want, you might be endangering yourself.

1. Face your partner from a distance of approximately five feet, with him fully knowing that you will execute a fake before your distance closure. Execute a fake or distraction of some sort (punch, kick, pointing, finger flick, etc.) Have your partner react by twisting, looking, moving, etc., and as soon as he does, spring forward and grab him in a cross wrist grab. Make your advance explosive and quick.

2. Repeat the exercise a number of times, but have your partner ignore the fake some, but not all, times. Only spring forward when your partner reacts. The purpose of this is to train yourself to be observant of your opponent's reaction and make split second decisions.

3. Repeat the exercise, but when you fake, have your partner advance, keeping you from carrying out your initial plan. Experiment with the possibility of grabbing him in a cross wrist grab anyway, even though your plans were thwarted. Thinking in concepts (unbalancing techniques), rather than in specific "cause and effect" techniques, will increase your chances of being successful. It's the end result that is important (that your opponent goes down and is rendered harmless) and not the exact means by which this is achieved.

## Physical / Mental Exercise

In theory, the throw from the cross wrist grab can also be used against a person trying to stab you to the mid-section with a knife. However, I am of the opinion that this is risky, because you will be pulling the knife toward you. Not only does it take great timing to intercept such an attack, a tiny mistake can be fatal. It is really no physical difference between intercepting an empty hand that is striking or reaching for you, or a hand wielding a weapon. There is, however, a *mental* difference. Try this with a partner:

1. Try to intercept your partner's hand when he is reaching for you empty handed. Work on a variety of speeds, incorporating footwork and angles.

2. Next, have your partner attempt to stab you with a training knife made of rubber. If you feel the slightest touch from the knife, it will simulate a severe cut that will at least halt your technique long enough to give your opponent the edge. How does this change your perception of how precise you must be with the technique?

3. Next, have both you and your partner grab training knives and move around in a confined area while attempting to stab each other. If the blade of the knife touches either one of you, the fight will be over for that person. How does it change your partner's attitude about his attack, when he knows that he is at risk of receiving a fatal wound?

---

## Safety Tips

1. When training with a weapon, wear goggles to protect against an accidental stab or scratch to the eye.

2. Use less contact than you would in a real scenario. Even a rubber knife has the capability to scratch, sting, and bruise, especially when contacting bare skin.

---

# Reverse Throw Using the Body as Leverage

Use this throw whenever there is an opportunity to wrap at least one of your arms around your opponent's body. For example:

1. As defense against a slashing knife attack or wide punch.

2. When you initiate the technique with a tackle.

If used against an inward slashing knife attack or a wide punch, first defend the attack by moving to the superior position away from opponent's centerline, or by bobbing and weaving under the attacking arm. Simultaneously close distance and wrap your arms around your opponent's body. You should be off to one side, and not right in front of him.

Note that any armed attack is extremely dangerous and difficult to defend against, and that no technique is foolproof. The concept we're working is defense against an attack that involves a wide swinging arm motion from the outside in. The purpose of this is to recognize a specific motion and give you the option of an unbalancing technique, whether your opponent is wielding a weapon or not.

If you are initiating the technique with a tackle, your gap closure must be quick and explosive, and preferably set up with some distracting move. Proceed as follows:

- When you have closed distance and achieved the body lock, step behind your opponent with the leg that is closest to his body. You are now hip to hip, with your position superior because of your arm across his body.

- Move your free hand up to his upper back or shoulder. This gives you two points of balance, allowing you to use the push-pull principle. Make sure that your hip is deep enough to join centers of gravity with your opponent. This allows a smaller person to throw a much larger adversary without a great deal of effort.

- Throw your opponent backward over your hip by pivoting your body diagonally downward. The throw will be more violent if you twist your opponent's body using the *push-pull* principle: push with the arm that is across the front of his body, and pull with the hand that is on the back of his shoulder, simultaneously applying a rotation to misalign his posture. If you have a hard time grabbing the shoulder itself, you can also grab your opponent's clothing. Or, as a variation, cup his chin with your hand and force his head to the rear.

- Your opponent will land on his side by your feet, facing away from you. Run to escape, or drop your knee onto his head and continue with another controlling technique.

## Points to Consider

1. If your opponent lands on his side, it is better if he is facing away from you than toward you. Not only does this take away his vision, it also limits the use of his hands and legs. In most of these reverse hip throws, your opponent will naturally land facing away from you.

2. Some people find the body throw more difficult than the throws we have previously discussed. This may be because you are not relying on the easy to use neck manipulation. To succeed with this throw, it is especially important that your and your opponent's centers of gravity become one and the same. If there is separation between the C.G.s, there will automatically be resistance to the throw. When working with the heavier body, the farther apart the C.G.s are, the more effort the throw requires, so don't allow a gap to form between you. Once your opponent starts going over your hip, allow his C.G. to separate from yours. Once it falls outside of the foundation of your feet, the throw will be certain. However, in order for you to maintain balance, your own C.G. must continue to fall above your foundation. Don't allow the weight of your opponent's body to drag you to the ground with him.

3. If using the takedown variation, the technique is identical, except that you are not stepping behind your opponent preparatory to the throw. A wide sweeping motion of your leg, with your forearm across his body and your other hand pulling on his arm or shoulder, provides the momentum for the takedown.

# Reverse Throw from Double Hand Shoulder Grab

Use this throw whenever there is an opportunity to grab your opponent's shoulders from the front, with one hand on each shoulder. For example:

1. As a defensive move trying to stop an opponent who is approaching you.

2. As an offensive move, where you are grabbing or shaking your opponent.

3. As an offensive move, where there is a need to get past your opponent, or to clear a narrow pathway.

If the opponent is approaching in a threatening manner, our natural tendency is to raise our hands and try to stop him from coming closer. Once you make contact with your adversary, act on the first touch concept and start the throw right away.

If you are grabbing and shaking your opponent, the move has probably escalated from a verbal argument. You might want to reconsider your options.

If it is necessary to clear a narrow pathway, like a hallway or a door that your opponent is blocking, close distance quickly, using your body momentum to bump him off balance. Proceed as follows:

**Note the push-pull against your opponent's shoulders to misalign his posture. Your hip and leg behind his will immobilize his foundation, allowing you to shift his center of gravity and join with yours.**

• When you have achieved the shoulder grab, step behind your opponent with the foot that is closest to his body. You are now hip to hip, facing opposite directions, with your position superior because of the grab.

- Throw your opponent backward over your hip by pivoting your body diagonally downward, simultaneously pulling with one hand and pushing with the other. Because your opponent's foundation is not allowed to move, the push-pull will misalign his posture and unbalance him. It helps if your opponent is already slightly off balance to the rear, and if he is wearing clothing that you can grab.

## Points to Consider

1. Using your whole forearm (not just your hand) pushing against your opponent's chest is effective for getting his weight to the rear before proceeding with the throw. Once your opponent is off balance, his strikes or counter-moves are less effective.

2. If using the takedown variation, the technique is identical, except that you are not stepping behind your opponent. A wide sweeping motion of your leg provides momentum for the takedown. As you can see, this throw is quite similar to the body throw discussed above.

## Reverse Throw from Wrist Lock

Use this throw whenever you have the opportunity to gain a lock on your opponent's wrist. For example:

1. When your opponent reaches out to grab you.

2. When your opponent comes at you with a stabbing knife attack.

3. After a lock-up around the neck.

If your opponent reaches out to grab you, intercept his hand while his focus is still on offense. A parry to the outside of his arm, followed by a quick grab of his wrist may work. It is difficult to catch the arm in mid-air and be successful with the grip. Parrying first, before grabbing, stalls your opponent's momentum and makes the grab easier.

If your opponent attacks with a knife, first block or parry the attack before closing distance to ensure safety against the blade. Take up the superior position to the side and slightly behind your opponent.

If your opponent grabs you in a lock-up around the neck, you have a little more time to pry one hand off. Proceed as follows:

**The outside wrist lock relies on two points of balance in the lock itself: the hand is bent toward your opponent, while simultaneously twisted to the outside through its full range of motion. This locks out the elbow, which, in turn, locks out the shoulder. Manipulating your opponent's body is now easy.**

  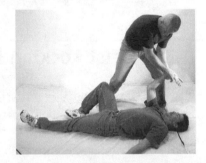

- When you have achieved the wrist lock, step behind your opponent with the foot that is closest to him until you are hip to hip, facing opposite directions, with your position superior because of the joint lock. Make sure that the wrist remains locked until the throw is complete.

- Throw your opponent backward over your hip by pivoting your body diagonally downward. The joint lock and the hip are your two points of balance. A quick twist of your body causes severe strain on the ligaments in your opponent's wrist and shoulder.

- Maintain control of the wrist both during the throw and after your opponent has landed on the ground. Continue control with the joint lock you have already established.

## Points to Consider

1. The reverse hip throw with a wrist lock is usually not done when you are the one initiating the attack. A wrist lock requires fine motor skills to apply, and is therefore difficult to attain unless your opponent is preoccupied.

2. Intercepting a violent attack, such as a knife stab or punch, and successfully gaining a wrist lock is difficult, very risky, and requires considerable knowledge and practice of wrist locking techniques. We will not explore wrist locks in detail in this book, but if you have prior knowledge of such techniques, this type of throw may prove useful.

3. If using the takedown variation, the technique is identical, except you will be sweeping your foot in a wide circle instead of stepping behind your opponent. Keep your opponent close to your center of gravity. He should feel the wrist lock throughout the technique.

## Wrist Locking Exercise

A properly applied wrist lock is so devastating because it goes against the natural movement of the joint, causing immediate and extreme pain. If the lock is intensified, the joint will dislocate or break. A properly applied joint lock immobilizes more than the joint it is applied to, and is therefore likely to give you immediate compliance. However, easy as it may sound, it takes considerable practice to correctly apply a lock against the wrist. Minute flaws in technique preclude you from attaining the desired effect. Try this:

1. Experiment with wrist locking techniques on a partner. Start by gently bending and twisting the wrist in all possible directions, while identifying the wrist's inherent weaknesses. Work the wrist slowly and with control, allowing your partner to tell you when you have achieved his pain threshold. Don't go any further.

2. When you have identified a technique that goes against the natural movement of the joint, and that appears to be effective as a wrist control technique, apply it until your partner alerts you of the point of pain. Experiment with minute changes in the lock, and identify whether these lessen or worsen the pain. This exercise is supposed to bring out understanding about the precision needed to succeed with a wrist lock.

# Thoughts on Throws

We have now looked at throws as defense against a number of attacks, including overhead strikes using a weapon, grabs around the neck with one or both hands, wild "bar brawling" swings, attempted grabs or punches, knife attacks, and situations where you decide to initiate the technique. But, as you can see, all of these throws are identical in principle:

1. You are facing the opposite direction of your opponent. This allows you to throw him rearward over your hip.

2. You have stepped behind him with the foot that is closest to his body. This immobilizes his foundation and keeps him from adjusting his center of gravity once he starts losing balance.

3. You are utilizing your hip as the balance point, and are using a diagonal downward twist of your body to shift your opponent's center of gravity and get the throw started.

4. You are using two points of balance and the push-pull principle. The two points of balance vary depending on your position and circumstances, but the principle remains the same.

5. Your opponent lands on his side by your feet, and is facing away from you. This gives you the opportunity to drop a knee press onto his head. Because he is on his side, he also has one arm exposed, allowing you to further control him.

The thing that should be learned from this is that regardless of the type of attack, the principles for executing the throw are limited and remain the same. This eliminates the need to learn a separate technique as a counter-measure for each possible attack.

But what about kicks? Can you defend and execute a throw against a kick? Look at the principles. If you have the opportunity to get hip to hip with your opponent, facing opposite directions, you can also utilize the rest of the principles of center of gravity, balance manipulation, and push-pull to execute a throw. So, the question to ask is not if a throw as defense against a kick is possible, but rather whether it is possible to close distance and get in position for the throw. As we have explored earlier, distance can be closed easiest on a round house kick, because it follows a circular arc and connects from the side. When closing distance on a front or side kick, you must either initiate your move prior to extension of your opponent's kick, or wait until after his kick has come to completion.

# Forward Throws

Most forward throws require you to be facing the same direction as your opponent. Forward throws can be a little trickier to execute than rearward throws for the following reasons:

1. When engaging your adversary, you are likely to initially be facing him, and therefore be facing the *opposite* direction. Positioning for the forward throw requires that you turn 180 degrees until your back is toward your opponent.

2. The unbalancing move itself may be more difficult, because your opponent's body has a natural forward bend at the waist and hips. You can therefore not take advantage of going against the natural movements of the joints.

However, an advantage of the forward throw is that you can execute it against blind attacks from the rear (rear choke or rear bear hug, for example). The forward throw can also be entered along your opponent's centerline between his arms, or from the side of his body, with one of your arms around his upper back.

The principles for the reverse and forward throws remain the same. You must utilize momentum (straight or circular), *torque* whenever possible, and two points of balance (usually your hip and some other part of your opponent's upper body anatomy). You must also keep your own body stabilized around your own center of gravity, and allow it to join with your opponent's center of gravity just prior to the throw, which means leaving no gap between your bodies. Just as with reverse throws, we will try to identify a specific movement in our opponent's attack, rather than a specific technique for each possible scenario.

## Lesson Objectives

At the end of this lesson, you should be familiar with the following throws:

1. Forward throw from single wrist grab
2. Forward throw from head lock
3. Forward throw as defense against a rear choke
4. Forward throw from double hand crossed neck manipulation
5. Forward throw from straight arm shoulder grab
6. Forward throw from guillotine choke

# Forward Throw from Single Wrist Grab

Use this throw whenever there is an opportunity to grab your opponent's wrist or arm in a straight wrist grab (same side). For example:

1. When your opponent reaches out to grab you.

2. After blocking or parrying a strike.

3. As defense against a slashing knife attack.

4. As an offensive move, where you initiate the technique.

If your opponent reaches out to grab you, intercept his arm in a straight wrist grab. Grab his right wrist with your left hand, or his left wrist with your right hand. You must anticipate the situation, so that you gain control by grabbing him before he has time to grab you. The moment you feel your hand connect with his wrist (first touch), step to close range along his centerline and turn until your back is toward your opponent and you are facing the same direction he is. Think of it as a dance step where you are swirling into his arms. Your hip should be touching his with no gap between your bodies. A gap creates slack, which must first be eliminated before the technique can take effect. Pull his arm diagonally across the front of your body. Your free hand can be placed around your opponent's upper arm.

**When you have turned to face the same direction as your opponent, you will actually have him in a cross wrist grab. This allows you to pull toward the centerline of your body, where your strength and balance are focused.**

If you are blocking or parrying a punch, your block or parry must be to the inside of your opponent's arm for this particular technique to work. The hand that is on the same side as your opponent's punching arm should do the blocking. Note that since you are working along your opponent's centerline, this does not necessarily place you in a superior position. On the contrary, a block to the outside of the arm would place you slightly toward your opponent's back, but you have to proceed with a different type of throw. After blocking, slide your hand down to your opponent's wrist. Step in and turn around until you are facing the same direction he is. Pull his arm diagonally across your body.

If this technique is used as defense against a slashing knife attack, your timing must be very good. It is recommended that you use a double forearm block to the inside of your opponent's arm. Note that the attack must be a wide slash that allows you access to the inside of the forearm. Tight "figure eight" slashes with the knife in the reverse grip are very difficult to block, and a press to the outside of the forearm might be a better alternative. We will look at this in Chapter 12.

Grab your opponent's wrist with the hand that is closest to his wrist, and grab his upper arm with your other hand. Step in and turn around until you are hip to hip facing the same direction. Pull your opponent's arm diagonally across your body.

If you are the one initiating the technique, you will have to reach for your opponent's wrist. The technique should therefore be set up with a distracting move. Once you have achieved the grip and turned to face the same direction as your opponent, proceed as follows:

- Throw your opponent forward over your hip by pulling his arm diagonally down across your body, simultaneously pivoting your body in a downward spiral. When you initiate the throw, push your hips back into your opponent with the intent of displacing his center of gravity with your own. If you simply pull on the arm with no movement in your hips, your opponent's inertia will cause you to struggle with the throw.

• Your opponent will land on his side or back. Proceed with a press by dropping your knee onto his head. Because you have control of his arm, you can also turn him to an inferior position on his stomach by using a controlling technique against the wrist and elbow. Of course, a third option is to let go of him and run.

## Points to Consider

1. When achieving the wrist grab, first pull your opponent forward to unbalance him. This acts as a distraction, momentarily making him struggle with his balance and taking his mind off the throw.

2. Your opponent's arm should be resting on your shoulder. This, along with your grip on his wrist, gives you two points of balance, with your hip acting as the stabilizing point and center of rotation.

3. If using the takedown variation, the technique is identical, except you will use a wide sweeping motion of your leg rather than a tight hip to hip throw.

## Blocking Exercise

Learning the mechanics of a block is not enough, unless you also have an understanding of what it takes to block an attack thrown with full intent. Try this:

1. Have your partner wear a forearm pad and swing at you with a wide slashing knife attack, using a rubber training knife. Start out slow and experiment with blocking the attack. Have your partner increase the speed and intensity of the attack. The purpose of this is to gain an understanding of how powerful your block must be in order to stop the attack.

2. When you add to this the element of uncertainty — you don't know exactly when or how your opponent is likely to attack — defending against the attack is more difficult. Have your opponent swing at you hard and fast. Force yourself to use enough power in your block to stop the attack.

# Forward Throw from Head Lock

Use this throw whenever there is an opportunity to grab your opponent around the neck in a head lock. For example:

1. When you have achieved a cross wrist grab and pulled your opponent diagonally toward you. This will position him with his back toward you.

2. When you initiate the technique from behind your opponent, as when coming to the rescue of another person.

If you use a grab to manipulate your opponent's position, your technique must be quick and forceful to avoid the risk of excessive resistance. Simultaneously to applying the head lock, position the foot closest to your opponent in front of his body, until you are hip to hip facing the same direction.

As with all techniques, the head lock must be *definite* to serve its intended purpose. Your arm should not be loose around your opponent's neck. Rather, squeeze his neck by clasping your hands tightly together. Note how your own body weight is forward.

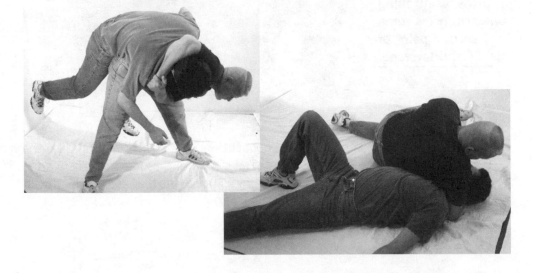

If you initiate the move from behind your opponent by coming to the rescue of another person, wrap your arm around his neck the way that is most natural for your position. Step in front of your opponent with the foot that is closest to him, until you are hip to hip facing the same direction. Proceed as follows:

- When you have achieved the head lock and are hip to hip with your opponent, throw him forward over your hip by pivoting your body in a downward spiral. Use his neck, combined with your hip, as leverage.

- The forward throw from the head lock works best if you keep control of your opponent's head and drop to the ground with him. Once your opponent starts going over your hip, you can also let go and allow him to fall. The disadvantage of this is that you have to re-establish control, if it is necessary to further subdue him on the ground.

Because your opponent remains in a tight head lock, this throw does not lend itself to a takedown variation. A variation of this throw is to wrap one of your arms around your opponent's back, with your free hand controlling one of his arms. You can now use his arm and upper back as a lever, with your hip as the pivot point.

**Your opponent's weight will be forward in the natural direction of the movement of his arms. Controlling one arm gives you a second point of balance and leverage.**

Note that having control of your opponent's arm is important to reduce the risk of him grabbing or striking you. The same is not necessarily true for the reverse throw, as your opponent's weight will be to the rear, making it difficult for him to execute a powerful grab or strike.

# Forward Throw as Defense Against a Rear Choke

This is one of the easiest and most effective escapes from a rear attack. Use this throw when your opponent has grabbed you around the neck in a choke (where he is attempting to cut the flow of blood to the brain) or if he simply places his arm around your neck with his elbow to the front. This places you in a natural position for a forward hip throw; you are automatically hip to hip with your opponent.

The moment he applies the rear choke, place your hand on his arm above his elbow for stabilization and to lessen the effect of the choke. Note that this technique does enable you to throw your opponent without even touching him. With a little practice, once you join centers of gravity with your opponent, the motion of your body alone will enable you to throw him. Proceed as follows:

- Reach up and grab your opponent's upper arm with one or both hands. This is a natural reaction, as we have a tendency to grab the arm that grabs us. If your opponent is very close, you can also reach straight back over your head and grab the back of your opponent's head.

- Tuck your body forward, so that your back is rounded (this is a natural reaction when sensing danger) and displace his center of gravity with your own. Twist diagonally toward your opposite leg. The twisting can be thought of as "taking a bow" or "looking behind you" and to the outside of the leg that is opposite of your opponent's grip.

- Throw your opponent forward over your hip by pulling on his arm and pivoting your body diagonally toward the ground. As he rolls over the top of your back, the arm around your neck will automatically extend and free you from the choke.

This throw can also be done against an opponent who is choking you from behind, or grabs you in a rear bear hug, when you are kneeling. The same technique and motion apply. As your opponent wraps his arm around your neck, place your hands on his arm above his elbow. Tuck your shoulder toward the opposite side (with a dynamic twist in your body). If he grabs you in a bear hug, reach back and over your head and grab his head, pulling it forward while rounding your back.

As you initiate the throw, pull your opponent's elbow toward your chest to lessen the choke and enable you to execute the throw. Once your opponent rolls over your back and shoulder, you may either let go and escape, or roll with him so that you land on top of him and perpendicular to his body. You can now move into an arm bar against his elbow. Make sure that your weight is not directly on top of his body, or a strong opponent may be able to unbalance you and throw you off.

**Make sure that your opponent's elbow is pointed toward you. If he can bend his arm, he may also be able to grab you around the neck anew.**

Note that the throw from a kneeling position provides a good place to start when training in throws. The body mechanics are identical for kneeling and standing, but the fall won't be quite as severe. If your partner is not skilled at taking a fall, the kneeling position will lessen the impact, allowing you to be dynamic with the technique – a skill that can later be applied to the standing throw.

## Points to Consider

1. When your opponent reaches around your neck, press your chin down toward your chest. This makes it more difficult for him to achieve a good choke and buys you time. In a throw, you want to bring your upper body forward anyway, and pressing your chin down naturally positions you for the throw.

2. It is very important that your body is tucked and your back is rounded. If your back is flat and you simply bend at the waist, you will give your opponent a platform to rest on. A rounded back will make him roll over the top of you.

3. This type of throw can also be used as defense against a head lock, with a slight variation. Instead of throwing your opponent over your back, throw him over your hip. But the motion of the technique is identical: tuck your body tight and twist toward your opposite leg.

## Forward Throw from Double Hand Crossed Neck Manipulation

Use this throw any time you have an opportunity to approach your opponent from the front, or any time you accidentally end up with your back turned partially toward your opponent. For example:

1. When your opponent attacks with a wide slashing knife attack, or with a wide punch (haymaker).

2. When your opponent reaches out to grab you.

3. When you initiate the technique from long range.

4. In a close range "push and shove," where you get turned partially away from your opponent.

If your opponent attacks with a knife slash or wide punch, block the attack to the inside of his arm with a double forearm block and step to close range along his centerline.

A grab is a little less threatening than a punch or weapon attack. If your opponent reaches out to grab you, the same principle applies, but you should preferably react before he has tightened his grip.

If you are the one initiating the technique, set it up with a distracting move first. Be careful not to walk into your opponent's strikes when you close distance.

If you are in a "push and shove," take advantage of the opportunity as the situation unfolds. You can apply this particular throw any time you end up with your back turned partially toward your opponent. Proceed as follows:

**The reason this is a "crossed" grab is, because if you grab prior to turning around, your arms will be crossed. When you have tuned your back toward your opponent, your arms will no longer be crossed. If you reach out to grab while you are in the process of turning, you only have to do what comes most naturally. Your mindset should simply be to grab your opponent around the neck with both hands.**

- As you are closing distance along your opponent's centerline, start turning with your back toward him. Simultaneously reach out and grab the back of his neck with both hands.

- You are now hip to hip with your opponent, facing the same direction, with your position superior because of your grip around his neck.

- Throw your opponent forward and diagonally over your hip by pivoting and tucking your body. Keep your elbows tight along your centerline.

- Your opponent will land on his side or back. Because both his hands are free, it is essential that you pin his head as soon as possible. Pinning the head allows you to gain a control hold and turn him over on his stomach.

## Points to Consider

1. It may seem as though any move that turns you with your back toward your opponent automatically places you in the inferior position. But this is true only if you lack knowledge or planning. In this particular case, your position is one of strength, because you also have control of your opponent's neck, which is an inherently weak part of his anatomy.

2. If using the takedown variation, sweep the foot that is on the opposite side of the grab in a large circle, simultaneously pivoting your body in a downward spiral. Your opponent will be falling around your body instead of over the top of your hip.

## Forward Throw from Straight Arm Shoulder Grab

Use this throw whenever your opponent places his hand on your shoulder, or if he is wrapping one arm around your neck from a position behind you.

When you feel your opponent's hand on your shoulder, reach up and grab his wrist with both hands. If his arm is wrapped around your neck, grab his thumb or a finger and pry it off. The fingers are inherently weak and a person's whole body can easily be manipulated through his little finger. Move his body close to yours, so that you can join your centers of gravity. Rather than pulling on his arm, try taking a step back until you feel your body against his. Proceed as follows:

- Turn your opponent's arm with the elbow down, and throw him forward over your hip by pulling on his arm and pivoting your body diagonally downward.

- Your opponent will land on his side or back. Since you still have control of his wrist, you are at an advantage. Use your grip to turn him to the inferior position on his stomach. Go against the natural movement of his joint by keeping his arm straight and placing your hand against the back of his elbow.

- When you have turned your opponent to his stomach, control him by dropping your knee onto his head, or by transferring into some other joint manipulation technique.

**Turn your opponent to his stomach by exerting pressure against the elbow. Drop your knee onto his head.**

## Points to Consider

1. Pull forward on your opponent's arm before initiating the throw to unbalance him and split his focus.

2. If possible, turn his arm with the elbow down. A good guide is his thumb. Whenever his thumb is pointing up, his elbow is down. This allows you to go against the natural movement of the elbow, giving you a good and inflexible lever. Your shoulder should be placed slightly above his elbow joint. This is your first point of balance, with the grip on his wrist your second point.

3. As you can see, this throw is similar to the throw from single wrist grab. The main difference is that your opponent's elbow is down, giving you a good lever and allowing you to use pain as a distraction.

## Forward Throw from Guillotine Choke

Note that all of the throws we have worked so far were done using your opponent's head or an arm as your high balance point. But what about a hair pull? If you were to grab your opponent's hair in an attempt to unbalance him, what type of grip would you use, and where would it be the strongest? Would you have more control to the front, top, or rear of your opponent's head? Experiment with a partner. Also experiment with grabbing your opponent's collar or shirtsleeve, and how to grip for maximum control.

Next, consider what to do if your opponent is rushing you in a full momentum tackle. If you can't side-step the attack, you may be forced to go down, but you should try to take your opponent with you. Rely on the momentum he has already built. As he comes toward you, wrap your arm over the back of his neck, push his head down and sit back or roll, throwing him forward over your body.

**This technique relies on your opponent's momentum, and on pushing his head down to direct the energy toward the ground. Note that even though this is a forward throw, you are facing the opposite direction of your opponent.**

You will both land on your backs. If your own back is rounded, you can utilize your opponent's momentum to pull you a full 360 degrees until you are straddling him. Get to your feet quickly, or stay on the ground and control him with a press.

The guillotine throw can also be used whenever there is an opportunity to grab your opponent around the neck in a guillotine choke from the side or front. For example:

1. When you free yourself from a lock-up and take up the superior position to the side of your opponent.

2. As an offensive move, where you are the one initiating the technique.

**Use *torque* on the elbow to get out of the lock-up.**

**Wrap your arm around your opponent's neck, and grab your wrist with your other hand.**

This technique can also be initiated before the lock-up, when your opponent reaches out to grab you around the neck. Through good timing, you can duck his grab and "bob and weave" to the superior position to the outside of his arm and slightly to the side of his body.

**A bob and weave is the ducking of your opponent's grab or punch in conjunction with sideways movement of your body.**

You can also initiate the technique before any attempted lock-up occurs, but you must then be dynamic and preferably set up the choke with another technique. When you have achieved the guillotine choke, proceed as follows:

**You will land on your back facing the opposite direction of your opponent. Continue with a choke from the position you are already in.**

- Bend your knees and roll onto your back, throwing your opponent forward over your body. Maintain the choke throughout the technique.

- Choke your opponent from your position on your back. Or attempt to use already established momentum and leverage on your opponent's neck to pull yourself to your knees.

## Points to Consider

1. Squeeze your biceps and forearm tight against the sides of your opponent's neck. This gives you good control with a psychological advantage. A tight squeeze against the carotid arteries can also restrict the blood flow to the brain, resulting in unconsciousness within a few seconds. The windpipe is very sensitive and, unless you intend to kill your opponent, try to keep it in the space of the crook of your arm rather than against your forearm.

2. When you wrap your arm around your opponent's neck, he will have a natural tendency to bring his hands up and grab your arm. As long as you act swiftly and continue his momentum, his center of gravity will shift forward of his foundation, and he will lack the strength and position to break your grip.

3. Because your opponent remains in a tight grip, this technique does not lend itself to a takedown variation.

## Carotid Choke Exercise

Experiencing the effects of a technique is invaluable from a self-defense standpoint because of the confidence it gives you. When studying self-defense, it is easy to fall into the trap of focusing only on how to apply our defense/offense on the other person. But much can be learned from experiencing it applied on ourselves in a controlled environment. Learning to defend against a strike, without knowing how to throw one, is only half of defense. Learning how to disarm an opponent, without having an understanding of the workings of a knife or firearm, is only half of defense. Likewise, learning how to apply a choke, without knowing what it feels like to have it applied on you, or without knowing the limitations of the technique, will only make you half as effective and may not work at all.

Because the guillotine choke is similar to the figure four choke, it is proper to discuss it at this time. If you lack the knowledge and education, don't experiment with this technique without proper supervision. Seek out a qualified martial arts instructor or officer of law enforcement, and have them demonstrate the technique correctly.

**Figure four choke.**

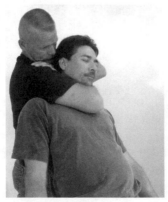 

1. A choke applied to the carotid arteries on the sides of the neck is highly effective at rendering your opponent unconscious and, because there is no pressure against the Adam's apple, the technique is generally harmless as long as you release the hold as soon as your opponent passes out.

2. The carotid arteries carry oxygenated blood to the brain. When having the choke demonstrated on you, have it applied slowly and gradually until you begin to feel the effects, which should only be a matter of a second or two. Let your partner or instructor know that you want out of the choke by tapping his arm or any other part of his body. There is no need to go to unconsciousness in order to get the point.

3. When the choke is released, you may experience a cough or difficulty talking for a few minutes. The next day, you may also feel a slight soreness in your throat, almost as if you were catching a cold. It should disappear within a day or two.

4. Learn how to apply the choke on others under your instructor's supervision. If done correctly, it requires very little muscular strength. Tighten the hold by hunching your shoulders forward. As with all self-defense techniques, it has to be *definite* (done with intent) in order to be effective. You won't have time to experiment or apply it "nicely" in a high threat situation.

# 11 Easy to Use Street Concepts

Being involved in a street confrontation is much different from fighting in a controlled martial arts environment. For one thing, the parameter of the fighting arena is not the same as what you are used to in sports. Many attacks are at least somewhat planned in advance, and are initiated by a person who has a specific objective in mind. Because of this, most attacks happen when the victim is at a distinct disadvantage. Attacks may also happen in a confined area where it is difficult to find an escape route.

Learning to defend yourself is not a matter of learning simple ABCs. You must also learn to anticipate problems that have not yet developed, and to see beyond the moment. What will happen if you do this rather than that? What if your opponent doesn't respond as anticipated? What if you apply a force that should have stopped your adversary, but he appears unharmed? How do you adjust to unanticipated problems or reactions? It is difficult to simulate an actual encounter in training with enough realism to make it as effective as the real encounter. For example, exactly how much force is needed to subdue an adversary? Perhaps even more important, exactly how much force is needed for him to subdue you?

You can train forever without contact and feel successful in the training hall, but when you have to suffer a loss early in a real encounter, how successful you are may be greatly influenced by how well you cope with this loss. However, even if you can't use your skill in training exactly the way you would in real life, training with any amount of contact or realism, no matter how small, is still valuable, because it gives you ideas that will further deepen your understanding and help prepare you for a real encounter. If nothing else, it opens your mind to more possibilities.

Just being aware of the areas where you are likely to become a victim may help you avoid an attack. Should an attack occur, however, you have a greater chance of prevailing if you have studied certain concepts beforehand.

## Lesson Objectives

At the end of this lesson, you should understand:

1. The different ways an attack can originate
2. How your clothing can help or hinder
3. The importance of knowing where your opponent's hands are
4. How to use strikes in combination with an unbalancing move
5. How to use kicks in combination with an unbalancing move
6. The value of instant pain
7. Easy to use finger holds

## How to Practice Your Art

Does self-defense have to be practiced at full speed in order to teach you about its effectiveness? Takedowns and throws are a little easier to practice at realistic speed than are strikes. This is because a strike thrown with full speed and intent is likely to hurt your training partner if it lands. The same is not true with takedowns and throws, as long as your partner is trained in proper falling techniques.

Once you have gained an understanding of your art, start to increase the speed of the attacks and defenses. If nothing else, this gives you a good indication of what you can or cannot do at your particular stage in training. The techniques must also be practiced against realistic resistance. This can be done after you have learned the basics of the techniques on a willing partner. In martial arts classes, you often see the defender blending effortlessly with the attacker's strike or grab attempt, and flawlessly using his opponent's momentum against him. I doubt this would happen in a real attack. You will be under so much adrenaline that it will be difficult to coordinate your moves to that precision even if you are highly skilled at your art, and a real attacker is not likely to throw a strike with a steady and predictable speed from several feet away. Blending with the motion of your opponent's full speed strike requires extremely fine timing, and if the strike is thrown from close range, you may not see it coming at all. If your opponent throws a combination instead of just one punch, you won't know what your best next move is.

I have often questioned how effective it is to teach a defensive strike or kick, or verbal de-escalation of an attack. Many techniques work well in theory, but I believe that it takes more than one good blow to finish an opponent intent on hurting you. When training for self-defense, you must understand how a technique thrown half-heartedly differs from one thrown with full intent of doing maximum damage. My feelings are that successful defense depends on how aggressive you (the victim) are. The word defense is, in itself, a bit misleading, because it makes us think of avoidance or blocking. In order to be a successful defender, you must have an offensive mind-set first; you must be mentally prepared to go the distance.

## The Stages of a Threat

When attacked on the street, one of two things will happen:

1. It will be a surprise attack, where you need to react immediately with whatever technique you have available.

2. The threat will build more slowly, where you have some time to plan for a proper counter-attack.

If you get forewarning of the attack, try to remove yourself from the situation before it escalates to a physical encounter. If somebody grabs or strikes you, you may need to engage your opponent for an unbalancing move, but this is not *always* necessary. If you have thought about possible scenarios beforehand, you may be able to de-escalate the situation, even if you have already been struck. Evaluate whether this is an isolated strike or grab, or whether there is a further threat to your safety. Granted, it is difficult to make such split second decisions in the midst of battle, so it helps to have done a considerable amount of thinking about possible scenarios beforehand. The nature of the threat can also be determined by knowing your opponent's reason for attacking you. Is he looking for a fight? Is he venting his anger? Is he out to rob or control you? If you can't de-escalate or get away, an unbalancing technique may be appropriate.

Once you have unbalanced your adversary, again try to get away. This may not always be possible, and you might decide to stay and subdue him on the ground. If you are the only one present, and there is little chance that somebody else will come and help you, a press to a sensitive part of your opponent's anatomy may not be enough, because as soon as you let up, your opponent may again try to hurt you. A sharp blow, a breaking or dislocation technique, or a choke to render him unconscious may be more appropriate.

If it becomes necessary to engage an adversary, your actions must be done with full intent. You must be committed and powerful. A strike, grab, or unbalancing move does not work off of "technique" alone. Even if your technique is very accurate, if there is no power or intent behind it, it will not work. In the training hall, you might see people fly yards away when you redirect the motion of their attack. But on the street, the attack is not likely to happen with so much obvious momentum that you can really send your opponents flying that far. And if you can see the attack coming from a mile away, you can just as easily flee it all together.

How much force should one use? In theory, the answer is simple: enough to subdue the attacker, without seriously injuring or killing him. In reality, however, the answer is not so simple. If the attack is unexpected, you have little knowledge of your attacker's motive, so it is more difficult to decide just how far to go. You must ensure your safety, until you no longer perceive a threat. The more you train in self-defense and chaotic situations, the easier it is to decide at the spur of the moment how much offense to use. This is because you train yourself to be more alert to situations that might require defense or offense, and so you are more aware of your own capabilities. If you train often, your mind will constantly be on self-preservation and, as a result, you will condition yourself to being ready with a moment's notice.

Another interesting issue is how to determine when it is necessary to defend yourself at all, especially if it is a surprise attack. If a friend or co-worker pushes you from behind in an act of playfulness, it would be inappropriate to turn around and throw him hard on the concrete floor. So, even if you're taken by surprise, you must still give yourself a moment to assess the situation.

## Your Clothing

The clothing you wear on the street will differ from what you wear in the martial arts training hall. Be aware of the limitations of blue jeans or a heavy winter coat. If you are wearing a scarf, it can be used against you in a choke, tie-up, or unbalancing move. Shoes or boots are good for kicking, since you don't have to worry about getting your toes or ankles busted. However, they also slow you down, particularly if they are bulky. It is a good idea to train in street clothes at least enough to make you aware of the limitations.

Your clothing and the way you stand can also restrict the use of your hands. For example, a verbal argument, if handled appropriately, will buy you time. But you must still be ready for the physical attack. If you cross your arms over your chest in an attempt to assume a non-threatening stance, don't interlace your arms. Cross them straight, so that you can quickly come off with a strike, grab, or defensive move, without running the risk of your hands getting entangled in your own arms. If you keep your hands in your pockets, make sure you can withdraw them fast before your opponent makes contact. Practice different non-threatening stances, and how to quickly step into position to throw a strike, kick, or unbalancing move.

## Establishing Contact

There is one part of your opponent's body that will usually present itself before any other, namely his hands. Think about it. If your opponent wants to grab your purse or wallet, he must use his hands. If he wants to rape you, he must use his hands. If he wants to strike you, grab you, or control you, he must use his hands. Even if he is wielding a knife or a gun, he must still use his hands. Many attackers want either your money or your body. It is unlikely that an opponent with such a motive will initiate the attack with kicks. Regardless of whether you are attacked from the front or rear, your best initial defense may be to establish contact with your opponent's hands or arms. This does a number of things:

1. Momentarily stalls his advance.

2. Gives you a clear perception of where his hands are.

3. Gives you the opportunity to follow with an unbalancing move.

Your first response is not to *control* your opponent's hands, but simply to *establish contact*, for any of the reasons listed above. Once you have stalled your opponent's advance by splitting his focus through contact with his hands, you can proceed with a softening or unbalancing move. Establish the superior position, preferably toward his back. Use your free hand(s) to manipulate your opponent's position, to keep him from striking or grabbing you, or from entering your zone of safety.

Throughout the confrontation, keep your escape routes in mind. If there is only one way out, your attacker will most likely approach you from that direction. Your first priority is now to switch positions with the attacker. If he reaches for you, try swatting his hand away from you and toward his centerline. This gives you outside superiority. Simultaneously run past your opponent. Even if you are unable to escape, this places you closer to the escape route and stalls your opponent's attack, giving you a window of opportunity for an unbalancing move.

If the escape path is narrow, you can also try pinning your opponent's arm to his body, simultaneously giving him a forceful push. Use momentum to stall his advance, and pin his upper arm as close to the elbow as possible. Pinning the lower arm is not as effective, as it still gives him mobility in the elbow.

## Striking on the Street

The weapons used on the street, as well as your choice of targets, are different from those used in sports martial arts. Although the ultimate aim is the unbalancing move, there are other ways to hurt an attacker and split his focus in preparation for the takedown. When striking your opponent, be prepared to take advantage of his reaction. The following is a recommendation of strikes that may be useful in a street situation, with possible follow-up unbalancing moves:

1. *The vertical punch.* This strike is faster and more likely to have your body weight behind it than a punch with your fist in the horizontal position. Since there is no rotation in the fist or elbow, the vertical punch can be thrown from close range and penetrate a tight defense. Some people also find this strike stronger than the horizontal punch, because of the way the bones in the forearm stay aligned and are kept from crossing. The primary target for the vertical punch is the nose. If your opponent's head snaps back on impact, initiate an immediate unbalancing move to the rear.

2. *The soft palm.* This strike is thrown with your arm and shoulder relaxed and your fingers spread, and should be "whipped" through the target. Targets for the soft palm are primarily the ears and nose. If thrown to the ears, consider a double soft palm strike, one to each ear. This could rupture your opponent's eardrums. Follow with an unbalancing move to your opponent's head (a rear takedown, or a forward or reverse throw). Throwing the soft palm to the body may distract your opponent, but won't do much damage unless thrown to a particularly sensitive target, like the kidneys or groin. If thrown to the body, use it as a set-up for a takedown.

3. *Finger pokes.* The primary target for the finger poke is the eye. The throat may also be a good target. To avoid injury to the fingers, use the "non-poking" fingers as support for the "poking" fingers. Try crossing two fingers for stability. If poking your opponent in the eye, you are likely to get an immediate reaction where he brings his hands up to his face. You can follow with any number of unbalancing moves, or run from the situation.

4. *The shuto.* This strike is thrown with the outside knife edge of your hand, and should be thrown to soft tissue areas like the throat. It may be especially effective if you can grab your opponent's hair and bend his head back to expose this target. Keep your fingers together to avoid injury to your hand, and strike with the "fleshy" part of your knife hand.

5. *The back fist.* This strike is thrown to the temples, jaw, or groin. A variation of the back fist is the outside hammer fist, where contact is made with the outside edge of your *closed* fist. This strike is stronger than the regular back fist, because of its direct alignment with your elbow. Striking to the groin with the back fist requires you to be in a position to your opponent's side, or directly in front of him with your back toward him. A forward throw, grabbing your opponent's neck, is a good unbalancing move to follow the back fist.

6. *The elbow strike.* This strike uses the bony portion of the elbow against a softer target (temple, nose). If striking with a hooking motion, contact with the tip of the elbow and approximately two inches down the forearm. Impacting with the tip alone increases the risk of the elbow simply "brushing" the target. The elbow strike can be thrown from close range when your opponent has grabbed you around the waist, or from longer range by initiating it with a step forward. When throwing the elbow from close range, use it mainly to split your opponent's focus and gain an opportunity to break free and continue with an unbalancing move. When throwing the elbow from long range, utilize your forward momentum to simultaneously knock your opponent off balance in preparation for the takedown.

7. *The forearm strike.* The outside or inside of the forearm is an effective weapon for striking the temples or bridge of nose. An inside forearm thrown to the body is generally used to knock the opponent back in preparation for an unbalancing move. The forearm strike can also be used preparatory to a choke. Let's explore the forearm strike in more detail.

# The Forearm Strike

When your opponent throws a strike or reaches out to grab you, side-step the attack to the outside of his body and parry his extended arm with your lead hand. Your rear forearm should come underneath his outstretched arm and against his throat, while you shuffle forward for momentum. As soon as your forearm makes contact with your opponent's throat or neck, step forward with the foot closest to your opponent, simultaneously wrapping your arm around his neck, clasping your hands together. Your position is superior to the outside of your opponent's attack line. Your foot is behind your opponent, giving you the option of immobilizing his foundation for a rear takedown or throw.

**The forearm strikes above the center of gravity, while you continue your momentum past your opponent. Note how his striking arm is pinned along with his neck. If the grip is strong, it will restrict the flow of oxygenated blood to the brain and could render your opponent unconscious.**

**Because you have immobilized the opponent's base, he is unable to shift his center of gravity to compensate for your control of his upper body. A forceful twist of your body, with your hip pushing into your opponent's center of gravity, will result in a rearward throw.**

Note that if your opponent has boxing skills, he may carry his non-striking hand high while he throws the punch or reaches for you. This presents a problem because you will not be able to wrap your forearm tightly against the arteries in his neck. Don't let it throw you off. Simply pin his arm against his neck with your arm and proceed with the takedown. However, it is unlikely that your opponent will act as a trained boxer and throw a clean punch with his non-striking hand high. It is more likely that he will loop the punch slightly wide, raising his elbow first and creating a bend in his arm with the elbow pointing to the outside. This gives you the opportunity to work along his centerline, as shown below.

From a slightly sideways stance, defend the strike or grab with the outside of your forearm, simultaneously striking with the outside of your other forearm to your opponent's throat or neck. Think of it as simply stretching your arms forward.

**As soon as you have evaded the attack, overhook both your opponent's arm and his neck. You can further unbalance him by kicking his leg and twisting his body to the side.**

**Note the overhook that gives you control of the striking arm.**

Wrap your arm around your opponent's neck, with your other arm over the top and around his arm above his elbow. Your hands should come together in front of your body. Your opponent will be in a guillotine choke with one of his arms pinned. Clasp your hands together and apply the choke, or initiate a throw or takedown. Because your opponent has little opportunity to move his head when he goes down, this can have a damaging effect on his neck.

# Kicking on the Street

Just like strikes, the kicks and targets you use on the street differ from those seen in sport karate, and should be learned with their effectiveness and ease of execution in mind. Limit your kicks to below the waist. Kicking above the waist may jeopardize your safety by exposing vital targets, such as the groin and legs. Kicking high is also time and energy consuming with a greater risk of losing your balance. Your primary kicking targets on the street are the knees and the groin. The following kicks may be useful in a street situation:

1. *Round house kick with the ball of your foot.* This kick can be thrown to the side or back of the knee, buckling the knee, causing the opponent to stumble or lose balance. This kick can also be used as an unbalancing move when thrown to the opponent's calf. If working from close range, impact with your shin to the calf or the back of the knee joint. Simultaneously grab your opponent's shoulder (clothing) or hair for an unbalancing move to the rear. You are utilizing two points of balance with wide separation, and to a natural bend in the body (back of knee). Whenever possible, use your opponent's clothing to brace yourself or reposition him for the kick.

**Reminder** **Time the grab and kick into one fluid motion. As you grab your opponent and position him to the side, your kick should already be starting forward.**

2. *Front kick.* The primary target for this kick is the groin. If the kick is thrown from very close range, you can impact with your shin instead of ball of foot. Think of it as simply lifting your leg straight up between your opponent's legs. This requires no chambering of your leg, making this a fast and easy to throw kick. The front kick with the ball of the foot can also be thrown to your opponent's knee or thigh, with the effect of his upper body coming forward. Because the ball of the foot covers a smaller surface area than the instep or bottom of the foot, slightly greater precision is needed.

3. *The knee.* The knee can be thrown in either round house or front kick motion to a multitude of targets (thigh, groin, abdomen, head if opponent is bent forward, and tailbone or small of back if coming to the rescue of another person). Impact with the kneecap itself. Because of the hard and small surface area of this weapon, it has

the capability to do great damage. Take advantage of your opponent's reaction with an unbalancing move.

4. *Side kick.* This kick must be thrown fast, with no or only minimal chambering of your body. Impact with the outside knife edge, or the bottom or heel of your foot. Only use the heel if it requires no turn in your body, as chambering for the kick may place you in a disadvantaged position. Aim the kick at the front of your opponent's shin, knee, or thigh. Think of the kick as a stomp, driving through the target hard. Because the opponent's legs are weaker than his heavier body, they will give against the force of the kick. The fact that you're wearing shoes will make the kick more effective. If kicking to the front of the knee or thigh, your opponent's upper body is likely to come forward, giving you the option to finish with an unbalancing move from the front or side.

5. *Stop kick.* This kick can be thrown to your opponent's thigh to stop his forward motion, giving you an opportunity to flee or launch an unbalancing move, or as an offensive technique to his ankle, shin, or knee. The stop kick is similar in concept to the side kick, but with the toes of the foot turned to the outside away from your centerline. The stop kick is potentially faster and, therefore, more effective than the side kick. Since the power is along your centerline, it allows you to keep your full body weight behind the kick without pivoting or adjusting your stance.

---

**Note how the stop kick allows you to keep your forward momentum without turning your body away from the attack.**

**Knife edge side kick**     **Stop kick**

A good way to practice the side and stop kick is to get some wooden boards about the length of your leg, and place them at an angle against a wall. Throw the side kick or stop kick to the "knee area" hard enough to make the boards shatter. This helps you develop your ability to kick through the target.

Remember that your first kick may not solicit the intended reaction. Your first kick may even miss the target entirely. You must therefore be prepared to use the first touch concept and immediately follow with your unbalancing move.

**Your Mindset**  **When kicking, try to project your power forward, eliminating the tendency to lean in the opposite direction of the kick.**

Any kick that you can throw when standing can be thrown from a position on the ground. Common mistakes when kicking from the ground include:

1. Failing to realize that your reach may be different than when standing, especially against an opponent who is standing.

2. Failing to place your body weight behind the kick. Increase momentum by pushing off against the ground and moving your body in the direction of the kick.

3. Failing to move to a more superior position, or go for a takedown, once the kick has stalled your opponent's advance or solicited a reaction.

## Takedown in Conjunction with Kicks from the Lock-Up

As the lock-up occurs (when your opponent interlaces his hands around your neck), use the *over and under* principle, with one of your arms over the top of your opponent's arm and the other underneath his arm for leverage. If you can't attain the over and under, try to dominate the inside (between your opponent's arms), with both your arms locked around his neck. Note that inside dominance gives you a better defense in the lock-up. If your opponent tries to strike you now, you can just spread your arms at the elbows, and he will have difficulty reaching you with his strikes. Inside dominance also gives you greater strength because your arms are along your centerline.

Prior to attempting the takedown, split your opponent's mind and body focus with kicks to his legs. Throwing a kick when in the lock-up may seem difficult because of your proximity to your opponent, but if you impact from the side with your shin, you can kick from any distance within the length of your leg. The kick doesn't have to be powerful enough to severely hurt your opponent, only enough to split his focus. Depending on your mobility, position, and distance, you can throw the kick to your opponent's thighs, calves, shins, or ankles. When kicking at close quarter range, throwing the kick at a diagonal angle upward eliminates the need to pivot your body for distance.

Next, look for an opportunity to unbalance your opponent. You might have to do this by feel. If your opponent places more weight on one foot, or moves his leg to protect it against your kicks, this is your window of opportunity. If your opponent's weight suddenly shifts to one foot, you might be able to start a circular takedown in the direction of his supporting leg.

**Think about this**

**When your opponent raises one foot off the ground, his foundation will narrow and he will unknowingly assist you with the takedown. Take advantage of it.**

## Creating Shock Value

An opportunity to escape from a grab can be created by attacking areas of your opponent's body that have a low threshold for pain, usually soft tissue areas, such as insides of upper arms or inside thighs. The inherently weak areas are also likely to create a reaction, including the groin, eyes, throat, and neck. The separation of your opponent's mind and body focus can be accomplished either by striking, biting, scratching, or pinching these areas.

The half-fist is a strike commonly used by karate practitioners. It differs from the normal fist in that your hand is only doubled up at the knuckles in your fingers, and not at those in your hand. The half-fist resembles a *tiger claw* with your fingers bent at the middle knuckle. Many karate practitioners use this strike to reach narrow spaces, such as the throat. However, one of the more effective uses for this weapon is not as a strike at all, but as a *pinch* to soft tissue areas with the intent of creating enough shock value to help you escape a control hold, lock, or choke.

**The half-fist can be used to pinch soft tissue areas.**

**When your opponent grabs you around the neck in an attempted lock-up, use the half-fist to pinch sensitive soft tissue on the inside of his upper arm. The moment you get a reaction, proceed with an unbalancing move.**

The pinch is most effective if you grab as *little* tissue as possible. A handful of love handles won't hurt nearly as much as one sixteenth of an inch of triceps. When pinching with the half-fist, use either all four fingers, or your index finger and thumb only. If you add a twist to the pinch, it is even more painful.

Experiment on yourself, or with a partner, to find all the soft tissue areas that create a reaction to the pinch. Explore the cheeks, sides of the neck, pectoral muscles, triceps, underarms, sides of the body, groin (you may not want to do this one for real), and inner thighs. Experiment with grabbing more or less tissue and note the effects of both. How does clothing restrict your use of the pinch? Experiment with your partner grabbing you in a variety of holds. Use the pinch to create a reaction, and immediately go for an unbalancing technique. Note that when using the pinch in training, you *will* get bruised.

An escape can be made more successful if you use one hand to attack your opponent's point of attack with a simultaneous distraction, such as a pinch, to a soft tissue area with your other hand. When your opponent reacts to the pinch, his grip will momentarily weaken, giving you control of his point of attack and an opportunity to go for an unbalancing move. Don't forget the use of your feet. If your hands are trapped, use the sole of your shoe to kick or rake down your opponent's shin.

Common mistakes when attempting an escape include failure to separate your opponent's mind and body focus, struggling with the point of attack without first applying a softening technique, and failing to follow up with an unbalancing technique.

## Three Points of Pain

The purpose of this concept is to split your opponent's mind and body focus and create an overload on his brain. For example, create one point of pain through a forearm press against your opponent's jaw line. A press is not in itself dangerous, but serves as a means of controlling your opponent through pain. However, a person who feels pain in only one place may be able to resist your attempt to control him. If you can produce two points of pain, a person will try to prioritize one point over the other. If point B hurts more than point A, he will ignore point A and focus on freeing himself from point B.

If you can produce three points of pain, most people's minds get overloaded. They will be unable to focus on any one point at a time, and will lose their ability to focus their efforts to free themselves from the pain.

Let's say that you apply a choke, utilizing the *three points of pain* principle. The first point of pain is the sides of your opponent's neck with your forearms squeezing his carotid arteries. The second point of pain is strain on his back when you start to take his balance to the rear. The third point of pain is from your hand wrapping around your opponent's head and covering his mouth and nose to restrict his breathing. Unbalancing your opponent when his focus is broken should now be easy.

**Think about this**

**How can I split my opponent's focus through three simultaneous points of pain?**

**Choking your opponent with your forearm and biceps, cutting off his air supply with your hand and taking his balance to the rear, is an example of the three points of pain concept.**

# Finger Locks

The only fine motor skills we will discuss in this book are finger locks. The fingers are small and relatively weak and easy to gain access to when your opponent has grabbed you. The fingers also have limited range of motion. Any finger or the thumb can be used to control your opponent. There are basically three types of finger locks:

1. Bending the fingers against their natural movement. For best effect, twist and bend simultaneously. The effectiveness of this hold comes from locking out the finger in two different directions.

2. Pulling the fingers apart from one another. The little finger is easiest to control this way, but any finger (or group of fingers) including the thumb can cause extreme pain through separation.

3. Compressing a flexed finger. The thumb works best for this, because it is exposed even when your opponent is making a fist. However, we will not spend time practicing this technique, as I feel the other two have a more immediate success rate.

**Reminder**

**Grab what is available. Encircle the thumb or finger with the whole palm of your hand.**

Experiment with grabbing any one of your partner's fingers and pulling to the side away from the other fingers, or bending it against its natural range of motion. **Be very careful when experimenting with your partner.** The range of motion of the fingers is limited to the side, not necessarily by the movement of the joint, but by the construction of the hand. Intensify your control by grabbing two adjacent fingers with opposite hands and pulling apart. Finger control can be used against a variety of grabs, including those from behind. If you know where your opponent's hands are, you also know where his fingers are, even if you can't see them. Any finger, or set of fingers, can be used to control your opponent.

Finger locks are primarily used to break free of a grip, lock-up, or choke. Since the fingers are inherently weak, it takes little force to cause extreme pain.

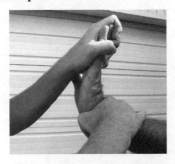

Grab any number of your opponent's fingers, one or all four, and bend, twist or pull them against their natural range of motion.

Bones can withstand pressure and blows better than they can withstand twisting. The ligaments that stabilize the joint are easily injured when stressed to the limits of the joint's range of motion.

**Think about this**

**The hands may be the greatest threat. If you break your opponent's fingers, he can't use his hands, and striking or grabbing is nearly impossible.**

Once you have gained control of a finger, use your whole body weight by stepping or driving with your hip or shoulder like you would when punching. Let's say that your opponent grabs your collar, shoulder, or neck from the front with one or both hands. His thumbs are now pointing toward your centerline. Grab his thumbs close to their base by encircling them with the palms of your hands. Forcefully pull the thumbs away from the fingers by pulling your elbows down and in toward your centerline. **Remember centerline strength.** Don't allow your elbows to point to the sides, as this makes it difficult to take full advantage of your body weight. Keeping your elbows close to your center of mass forces your opponent to drop to his knees instead of just stepping back. You have therefore accomplished a takedown through finger control. Crouch forward slightly and drop your body weight with the technique.

**Thumb control with body weight as defense to a front choke.**

Next, let's say that your opponent grabs you with both hands around the neck from behind. His little fingers will be to the front and closer than his thumbs to your center of gravity. Bring both your hands up and encircle his little fingers with your palms. Use a forceful outward pull to spread his little fingers from the other fingers. Rather than thinking in terms of pulling with your arms, think in terms of centerline strength. By bringing your elbows closer to your centerline, your hands, which are around your opponent's fingers, automatically move out to the sides, causing separation between his fingers. This can also be thought of in terms of the push-pull principle, where one part of your body is helping the other. When bringing your elbows toward your centerline, you are not relying on the strength in your arms alone, but also on the strength of your whole body.

If your opponent grabs you around the waist from behind, the same principle applies. Go for his little fingers and bend them against their natural movement. Grabbing the fingers and spreading them apart through a downward pull also works. Grabbing the thumbs and bending them against their natural movement is a third option.

Once you have freed yourself from the grip, control your opponent by his little finger alone. You can also let go of one of his hands to establish the superior position easier. Force your adversary to the ground by using a second point of balance on his elbow.

## Putting it All Together

Most people have the ability to excel at several martial arts, as long as these arts are practiced isolated from one another. For example, you might be a really good karate practitioner, or a really good boxer, in addition to being a really good grappler. It's when we try to combine the arts that we run into difficulties in fluidity (our ability to flow naturally from one art to another), because it requires "shifting gears." When we wrestle, we tend to get trapped in the pattern of wrestling, with all of its moves and concepts. Likewise, when we strike or kick, we tend to get trapped in the pattern of long range fighting and avoiding clinching or going down with our opponent. The same can be said for shifting from defense to offense, and vice versa. When practicing for the street, consider the following scenarios, and then make up more on your own:

1. Opponent throws a round house kick which you trap in the crook of your arm. Pinch the inside of his thigh hard with a half-fist, then strike with that same hand with an open palm to his hear, simulta-

neously lifting up on your opponent's leg and stepping forward for a rear unbalancing move.

2. Opponent grabs your lapel. Grab his little finger and bend it back against the natural movement of the joint. Throw a front kick to his groin, or to his face if he is bent over. Keep control of his little finger and continue pressing back and toward the ground, adding a twisting motion to the outside. Turn your opponent to his stomach through control of his finger, and drop a knee press onto his head.

3. Initiate the attack by throwing a forearm strike to your opponent's chest, relying on a great deal of forward momentum. Step behind your opponent's leg until you are hip to hip, facing the opposite direction. Move your hand up to your opponent's face, covering his face with your hand like a "suction cup." Continue tilting his head back and throw him to the rear over your hip.

4. Opponent comes toward you in a threatening manner, and you're trapped and can't escape the opposite direction. Before he is within reach to grab you, shoot at his lower legs, driving your momentum through until he hits the ground. Grab one of his feet by the heel and toes, twisting his foot forcefully toward his centerline to turn him to his stomach. The moment he tries to get back to his feet, throw a front kick aimed at his center of gravity to unbalance him a second time.

5. Opponent is straddling you on the ground. Reach out and grab the stick that is lying within reach. Swing it around the back of your opponent's head and grab onto it with your other hand as well. Roll the stick across your opponent's forehead and down the bridge of his nose, while pressing back forcefully. When your opponent raises his body up, drive your foot into his groin, simultaneously rolling onto your side and unbalancing him. Roll the stick down to his throat and, with you in the top position, continue pressing hard.

# 12 Knife Defense Unbalancing Moves

Being in a position where you are forced to go empty handed against a bladed weapon is always risky. When training in knife defense, it is easy to get trapped in an incorrect concept of time. The time it takes for you to react when an assailant is closing distance is much longer than we tend to think, and attacks happen faster than we would like to admit. If the assailant initiates his attack from a distance of ten feet, you are not likely to have time to get out of the way, and even less likely to pull off a fancy intercept technique with a complicated joint lock. In a high threat situation, you will end up the way you end up. You should therefore focus on developing a response in your opponent to buy time until you can effectively engage him.

An opponent with a knife may intend to control you, or he may intend to kill you. If your assailant is out to kill you, how definite must your defense be in order for you to walk away?

## Lesson Objectives

At the end of this lesson, you should understand:

1. Why going against the knife is one of the most dangerous of all situations
2. How to recognize a threat and the type of knife attack that is likely to follow
3. Possible ways to defend against the knife, and how to unbalance an adversary from an outside or inside position
4. How to unbalance an adversary when on your back
5. What realistic practice entails
6. The benefits of knowing how to use the knife offensively

## An Exercise in Futility

Going up against a knife is extremely risky, no matter how well trained you are. When confronted with a knife attack, safety is either in distance or in closeness. The worst possible distance is the "normal" fighting range (mid-range, about three feet from your assailant). If you can increase the distance to where your opponent is unable to reach you with the knife, it may get you to temporary safety. Likewise, if you can decrease the distance so that you are smothering your opponent's movement, it may allow you to unbalance or disarm him. We often don't think that safety can be in closeness. In order to unbalance your opponent, you must get close. However, the bad news is that when confronted with a skilled knife attacker set on killing you, it is almost impossible to survive the attack. The moves will happen so fast that even if you can fend off one or two strikes, you will get cut or killed by subsequent attempts. The reason we even explore this is to give you a slim opportunity to do the best with your situation.

**Reminder**

**When the attack is done with intent, your chances for survival are very slim.**

If you have any experience at all in a contact sport, you know that taking one good strike or kick, even though it may be painful, is not likely to end the fight or kill you. This bit of knowledge gives you confidence in your survival ability. Participating in full contact martial arts training, even if wearing protective equipment (gloves, shin guards, head gear), is good conditioning for building confidence to take a strike or kick. Now, let's assume that you know that your opponent is armed with a knife, and that one faulty move on your part will most likely mean death or severe injury. Will you be more cautious with the techniques you execute? The distance you keep? Your timing? Even though nothing else has changed, the way you approach the situation is different when your life is at stake.

## Recognizing the Attack

The knife can be held in the front or rear hand, and in the forward or reverse grip. The skilled attacker can also switch hands and grips quickly. However, all strikes can be done from two major hand positions only (with slight variations): palm up and palm down. The palm up position is generally utilized when stabbing from the forward grip (this can also be a partial palm up position), in an inward slash from the forward grip, or in an outward slash from the reverse grip. The palm down position is generally utilized in an outward slash from the forward grip, or in an inward slash from the reverse grip.

**Forward grip**

**Reverse grip**

**Forward grip, outward slash, palm down.**

**Reverse grip, inward slash, palm down.**

**The knife can also be a stabbing weapon when held in the reverse grip.**

Competent attackers don't necessarily show their weapon. If the fighter conceals his hand, it might be an indication that he is holding a knife. If your opponent has concealed the knife, he is likely to go beyond using it merely as a threat.

**A knife in the reverse grip can be concealed with the forearm.**

A person wielding a knife is usually waiting for the right moment to strike. He is likely to be nervous and on a high emotional level. Giving the attacker a perceived opportunity to commit may help you utilize the moment of first touch. A sudden, false move on your part can get the attacker to commit.

## Defending Against a Tight Slash with the Knife

Remember that it is your opponent's hands that are likely to kill you; this is where the knife is. Even if you can't see a knife in his hand, it may still be present and concealed through the reverse grip. This is one reason why it is important to keep track of where his hands are. Your opponent is also likely to attack high to the head, neck, or body, rather than to the legs. A workable defense might therefore be to shoot at his lower legs and go for a takedown.

Ideally, any defense against a bladed weapon should happen at the earliest stage of the attack. Initiate your move before your opponent has an opportunity to close distance. First, identify the type of attack that is likely to follow. If he is holding the knife in the forward grip, you are most likely looking at a stabbing attack. If he is holding the knife in the reverse grip, you are most likely looking at a slashing attack. However, it is possible to do an overhead or sideways stab from the reverse grip. It is also possible to do an inward or outward slash from the forward grip.

Let's assume that you have identified that it is likely to be a slashing attack. When defending this type of attack, whether from the forward or reverse grip, you must either distance yourself enough for the blade to miss, or work from a superior position outside of the attacker's arm. Moving toward his centerline only works if the slash is thrown wide. If the attacker engages in quick slashes with his arm bent at the elbow, it is more difficult to move inside of the attack without getting cut.

Note that tight slashing attacks are very fast and usually follow a figure eight pattern, where your opponent can easily execute several cuts per second. A skilled opponent will use tight moves and avoid extending his arm prematurely for you to grab. A slashing attack that comes wide is a little easier to defend against. When confronted with a knife, do what you have to, but remember that no matter how skilled a martial artist you are, when going empty handed against the blade, the odds are not in your favor.

 **Reminder** **Although it is not likely that a small person will attack a bigger person empty handed, the knife can be a great equalizer for the smaller person.**

If you are going empty handed against the blade, and you have the benefit of size (as shown on the next page), use it to create momentum for a takedown. Your window of opportunity is the moment your opponent misses with the blade. This is easier to time if you can draw the attack with a sudden, unexpected move. When your opponent lunges, step back and allow the attack to miss. Remember that it takes time to reset the body's balance after moving to the rear. However, inducing the attack places you in charge with a preplanned defense. Immediately step forward and pin the weapon arm against the opponent's body. Try to pin above the elbow to decrease the mobility in his arm. Use your body momentum to continue pressing back until your opponent is off balance. Then use your free hand to execute a rearward takedown through upper body or head manipulation in conjunction with a natural bend in his body. This type of defense places you to the outside of your opponent's centerline and in a superior position toward his back.

When pinning your opponent's arm, don't let a gap form between you. If you push against the back of the arm only, you may accomplish your initial objective of not getting cut, but your opponent is likely to come back with a second attack. Keep your own arms bent and push with enough forward momentum to jam his arm into his body.

Evade the attack.

Step forward to jam the weapon arm against the opponent's body.

Deliver a kick to the back of the knee, while shifting his center of gravity to the rear.

Stay with the technique after the initial tie-up. If you miss your opponent's arm, or if your grip slips, use your shoulder combined with body momentum to press his arm into his body.

Right. The opponent's arm is pressed into his body and he is beginning to lose balance.

**Wrong. The gap is too big, giving the opponent the opportunity to keep his balance and launch a counter-attack.**

You can also wait until your opponent is within a few feet of you. This works best if he closes distance methodically. Explode forward and at a slight angle to the outside, and engage his arm against the elbow. Push his arm toward his body. If your momentum is sufficient, this will control the knife wielding hand and move your opponent off balance. Proceed with a takedown before he has the opportunity to regain his composure. When your opponent hits the ground, turn and run, or drop a knee press onto his head. If it doesn't require overextending your center of gravity, try to gain control of the knife.

Note that your intent is not to gain initial control of the knife, as this requires fine motor skills and superb timing, where one mistake can be fatal. Rather, control your opponent's body and balance, which, in turn, controls the knife.

Even if your body mechanics are correct, a takedown may fail because you give your opponent time to make adjustments in his center of gravity. Any takedown is manyfold more effective if you can disturb your opponent's balance first. You can then afford a little "sloppiness" in the technique itself.

**Think about this**

**Your window of opportunity may be when your opponent's focus is distracted, and before he has closed distance (in the middle of a conversation, for example).**

# Defending Against a Stab or Wide Slash with the Knife

Defend against a wide slash by moving in and blocking to the inside of your opponent's forearm. The wider the attack, the easier this is. Use both of your arms to reinforce the block. Proceed with a single arm forward hip throw. Act on first touch. The pause between blocking and throwing should be minimal.

**Double-block a wide slash to the inside of the arm. Proceed with a forward throw, pushing your hips into your opponent and using the attacking arm as leverage.**

Defend against a straight stab by moving off the attack line and parrying to the outside of your opponent's arm, and moving in with a head manipulation takedown. If you manage to grip your opponent's knife wielding arm, you must act on it immediately. Delaying the unbalancing move even briefly may enable your opponent to wrestle out of the hold. The best unbalancing move is a violent throw. When your opponent is thrown, his focus will momentarily shift from the attack to his need to catch himself from the fall.

If you fail to act with a throw, go with the motion of your opponent's force, pushing his arm toward him and into his body. The move must be forceful with the intent of unbalancing him to the rear. Use your free hand for a neck manipulation takedown and, if possible, trip him by stepping behind his leg.

# Knife Blocking Exercise

When blocking a knife attack, where on your opponent's arm should you block? How should your timing be? How definite must your block be?

1. Experiment with attacks from different angles, with your partner holding the knife in either the forward and reverse grip. Can you use both hands to block or redirect the attack?

2. Experiment with working both from around your opponent's back and along his centerline. Can you follow up with a strike or disarming technique? How realistic is it? What are your targets?

Anything that can be used as a barrier, or any object that allows you to block or strike is beneficial. When the attack is imminent, if you have the time to take off your shirt or jacket and wrap it around your arm, you can use this arm to ward off the attack while closing distance for the takedown.

# Offense vs. Defense

When confronted with an armed attacker, it is generally better to act than to react. Our natural tendency is to shy away from the attack. But this places you in the inferior position already from the start. It is difficult to defend yourself effectively when you are backpedaling, with distance between you and your opponent rapidly decreasing. Your opponent knows that the knife is a high threat, and he is not expecting you to come after him empty handed. When you take the offensive stand, you place him in the mentally inferior position. Note that I'm not suggesting that you "walk into the attack," or that you stay and fight if you can get away. What I'm saying is that the person with the offensive mind-set is in better control of the situation and a step ahead of his opponent in timing and strategy.

Note that a natural reaction, when the opponent attacks, is to raise the arms in front of your face. Be aware of that this makes your arms and wrists targets for the knife. If you must get cut, try to take the cut on the outside of your forearms, rather than on the inside of your wrists. What other parts of your body can best withstand cuts? How can you use these parts to shield your more vital targets? Even a superficial cut can cause severe bleeding and shock. A common mistake when faced with an armed opponent is to get blinded by the weapon and forget your other options. Try to mentally condition yourself to fight as long as you need to in order to survive, regardless of your injuries.

This requires a lot of thought and visualization of possible attacks.

**Although a surface slash is generally less dangerous than a stab, a slash may cause a lot of bleeding.**

Think about this

## Using a Weapon in the Environment

Use any weapon you can find from your surroundings to guard against the knife. A good weapon is a regular chair. Hold the chair with the legs pointing toward your opponent, using it to ward off his advance or parrying and striking his knife wielding hand. Experiment with moving the chair in a figure eight pattern, simultaneously walking forward. A quick x-ing pattern with the legs of the chair, contacting your opponent's wrists or forearms, may help dislodge the knife from his hand.

**A chair can be an effective defense against the knife. Strike to the bones in your opponent's wrist, while keeping sufficient distance from the knife.**

Note that although the chair is effective against a knife wielding assailant, it is not necessarily so against an empty handed attacker. Your opponent is not likely to give up (or put away) his knife, and grabbing the chair with one hand is not likely to give him the leverage he needs. However, an empty handed assailant can grab the legs of the chair with both hands and take it from you. If your opponent grabs the chair with one or both hands, use a sharp and quick move to break the grip. This allows you to use his inertia (resistance to change) against him. If he is resisting on the linear plane, move the chair circular, and vice versa. If he grabs only one leg, twist the chair against the natural movement of the thumb to break his grip. Treat the situation as if the chair were a stick, using the push-pull principle and torque to twist it from his grip.

# Reversing Positions on the Ground

All fights that end with a knife attack don't start with a knife attack. How the fight starts or ends could depend on your opponent's motives. If his motive is to kill you, he will most likely be fully committed to attacking with the knife. If his motive is to get you to submit, whether for money or rape, the knife might be used primarily as a threatening device. Let's say that your opponent's motive is rape. When approaching you, he may have the knife hidden in his waistband because, in order to rape you, he must first take you down, which is difficult unless he has both hands free. The encounter may therefore appear empty handed, and then escalate to a weapon attack later, depending on whether you submit or not.

Don't discount the female attacker. An enraged female armed with a knife can be lethal. Let's say that your female opponent has taken you down, intent on harming you with the knife, and that she is either straddling you or is between your legs. It is of utmost importance to avoid getting stabbed or cut, but fighting power with power is a bad idea, even if you are bigger or muscularly stronger. If the opponent is between your legs and attempts to stab:

1. Grab her wrist with both hands and parry the arm slightly off the centerline and to the side of your head. You are not opposing power with power. Rather, you are relying on the force behind your opponent's attack to make the attack miss.

2. When the knife misses and your opponent is unbalanced forward, immediately swing the leg on the same side as the knife wielding hand around the front of your opponent's neck.

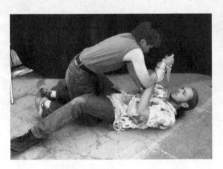 

3. Use the strength in your leg against her weaker neck and higher center of gravity to unbalance her to the rear. Keep your grip on her arm.

4. When she loses balance and falls onto her back, her knife wielding arm will be between your legs. Apply pressure against the elbow by raising your hips and turning her elbow toward the ground.

Next, let's say that your opponent is straddling you when she attempts to stab:

1. Grab her wrist with both hands and parry the arm slightly off the centerline and to the side of your head

2. When your opponent's upper body comes forward, grab her chin with your free hand and twist her head to the side and back. This will start unbalancing her to the side.

3. Use her higher center of gravity to pull you along until your positions are reversed. You will end up between her legs.

4. Continue turning her head and apply a forearm press. You can also reinforce with a knee press to the groin, pubic bone, or inner thigh.

Note that if you are the female, and you have gained access to a knife that you are trying to use against an aggressive male assailant, he can turn the situation to his advantage with an unbalancing move against you. If it can be helped, don't go to the ground with your opponent.

## Using the Knife Offensively

If you carry a knife for self-defense, be prepared to take the offensive stand. Knife fighting occurs at very close range, even face to face with your adversary. Do you have the emotional capacity to injure or kill with the knife? It is important to remember that a weapon is likely to escalate an encounter. Using a weapon should not be resorted to unless absolutely necessary.

Once you learn to use the knife offensively, your chances for survival in an attack, armed or unarmed, increase. Most of this is due to the fact that your mind-set about defense has changed. Instead of trying to time a parry, block, or movement to an adversary who is set on killing you, you will now take the offensive stand and do whatever necessary to render him harmless. Learning offense teaches you about the limitations of the weapon; it opens your eyes to what you can and cannot do, and how likely or unlikely you are to prevail against an armed attacker.

**Think about this**

Training with a weapon, even if you don't intend to carry one, can make you more confident against an armed attacker. Training with a weapon helps you gain an understanding of the uses and limitations of that weapon.

If both you and your opponent are armed, the treat level will again increase. You will both be a little more cautious before lunging forward. A single mistake in timing or distance could mean the difference between life and death. If you have a knife, and your opponent also has a knife, your positions are equal. Because the knife is so devastating, your opponent may opt not to fight once you display your weapon. In fact, what initially seemed like an escalation of the encounter due to the knives, may actually be a de-escalation. Try to talk your way out of the fight by reminding your opponent that he, too, has a lot to lose. Train with fake rubber knives and consider how the situation changes when both you and your partner are at risk of getting cut.

## Five Principles

In general, an armed attacker has the advantage over an unarmed defender. In any weapon attack, it is important to keep moving off the attack line, or try to get something between yourself and the attacker. In a knife encounter, a great distance is preferred initially. However, keep in mind that most people can cover 20 feet in less than a second. If possible find something in the vicinity that can be used as a weapon.

Because it is so difficult to defend against a true knife attack, you should focus on a few useful principles rather than on many complex techniques.

1. First, as discussed earlier, you must be aware of where your opponent's hands are at all times, because that's where the knife is.

2. Second, when the knife attack is inevitable, it is better to initiate than to wait for a move that you will have to react to. Your legs are longer than your arms, so if using a set-up for your gap closure, initiate with a kick.

3. Third, if you can get your opponent to move back while controlling his knife wielding hand, it will be difficult for him to launch an effective attack.

4. Fourth, look at stealing your opponent's balance as soon as possible prior to or after the initial tie-up. When you have split your opponent's focus, use momentum to close distance and knock him off balance.

5. Fifth, if your first attempt at controlling the attacker fails, you will most certainly get cut, or even lose your life. Prepare mentally for a possible cut, so that you can control your emotions if it happens, and continue doing your utmost to end the encounter.

# 13     Scenario Analysis

How important is strength? If you have your much bigger opponent in a figure four choke, and he tries to rip your arms apart, are you able to unbalance him or hold on until he passes out? Although the figure four choke is sometimes said to be foolproof, if it isn't applied tightly enough to cut off the blood to the brain, it will not work as quickly as intended. When your opponent struggles, the hold is likely to lessen, allowing him to retain consciousness. Can a 120 pound person be successful with this technique against a 220 pound assailant? Just how important is physical strength in a chaotic situation?

I have come across martial artists telling me to "use your opponent's motion to your advantage," or "take the path of least resistance," or "go with a push or a pull," or "don't tense." I, myself, am guilty of giving the same advice. But, once you start to experiment, you will find that this is easier said than done. The importance of most of the exercises in this book is not to develop absolute proficiency with the techniques, but to discover how you will react when under threat, and what you truly are able to do. If you are afraid, you will tense, even if you don't want to. When your body doesn't react as desired, can you still use these techniques? Or to what extent can you still use them? These are the questions you need to ask yourself. If a technique is only useful when you are in a relaxed state, it will probably not be very useful in a self-defense situation. I also often hear that you shouldn't show your fear. But fear can have a sudden onset. A person can start to shake uncontrollably or be unable to speak clearly and calmly, no matter how hard he tries not to show his fear. At the writing of this book, I have completed fifteen years of everyday study in martial arts, and a lot of it has been under the pressure of fear. I train in a full-contact art, and every time I step into the ring to spar, I know that I will get hit. When up against an unknown fighter, I always feel fear, although at this point I think I seldom show it. However, if suddenly attacked on the street where my life was threatened, I believe it would be difficult not to show my fear. I believe it is important to accept fear as part of who you are, and then try to harness it to your advantage.

The purpose of the following discussions is not to convince you of either this or that, but to make you think about these issues and, hopefully, experiment to gain insight into what it really takes to stop an attacker.

## Lesson Objectives

At the end of this lesson, you should understand:

1. How a real attack affects your nervous system and steals your hand/ eye coordination
2. How far you are willing to go when defending yourself
3. The differences in mind-set between a stand-up fighter and grappler
4. How studying the concepts can help you
5. How do deal with a variety of scenarios, how your planned defense can fail, and how to adapt
6. That some assailants are smaller than you, are female, and might use a weapon as an equalizer

## On the Chaos of an Attack

Get with a partner and preplan a defense against a specific attack. For example, have your partner reach out to grab you with his left hand, while planning to punch you with his right. Come up with a defensive/offensive set of moves against this technique. For example:

1. Intercept and grab the wrist of your opponent's grabbing hand.
2. Block the punch he is about to throw at you, and kick him in the groin to distract him.
3. Take him off balance using any takedown you have learned.

Practice the technique in slow motion a few times. Now have your partner speed up (but stopping short on the strike, in case you fail to block it). If you cannot pull off the entire technique against this greater speed, for the purpose of this exercise, it has failed.

If you have studied a martial art that requires specific techniques for specific defenses, have a partner attack you in any manner without giving the attack away. Respond with the specific technique the art calls for. You may have done a similar exercise in class and felt it was successful; however, the difference now is that your partner is of the mind-set that he will take the fight to the end. In other words, he will not stand there and let you finish after the first blows have been exchanged. He will be aggressive, force his momentum on you, and stifle your techniques. Even in controlled sparring, the weaknesses of having trained in specific techniques can often be seen. Because free sparring is at least somewhat unpredictable, you cannot prepare which defenses to use ahead of time. This often makes it seem as though the techniques you learn in class and the free sparring you do are two separate martial arts.

We usually try to defend the technique. When a technique fails, we have a tendency to say that we should have done this or we should have done that. Of course, the options are many, but it is almost impossible to foresee every single move in a stressful situation. A technique can fail in a split second, and then it is too late to talk about the "should haves."

Now, let's say that you don't know what kind of technique your partner will throw, you only know how you intend to defend against it: by grabbing his wrist, blocking his strike (if it's there), softening him up, and taking him down. Have him attack you with considerable speed. How successful were you? Did you have time to use your planned defense? Even if you managed to get a good grip on your opponent's arm, did you have time and ability to put him on the ground before he threw another strike? Remember, nobody will cooperate on the street, and the reason we experiment with this is to gain an understanding of how difficult it is to pre-plan a defense and use it successfully under stress in real time.

If you add to this a weapon in your partner's hand (a knife, stick, or gun), the technique is even more difficult to pull off because of the added stress, where a miss can mean the difference between life and death. Much of whether a defensive technique works or not also has to do with how enraged the attacker is. If his attitude is, "I don't care what happens, I'm going to kill you," you must succeed with your strike or unbalancing technique on the first try.

Finally, consider your own attitude. If it is one of rage, you will be more difficult to stop or take advantage of than if you are timid. If you are a mellow person, it may be difficult to imagine getting so outraged that you will actually kill or seriously hurt another person, even if your own life is at stake. But if we involve a loved one in the scenario, our attitudes tend to change. What if it were your mother, or your spouse, or your child that was under attack, and the only way you could keep them from getting killed was to attack the attacker and seriously hurt him? Would you still think it too outside of your personality to engage in battle?

# Is it Ethical to Kill in Self-Defense?

As far as your moral obligations go, it is important to know where you stand on these issues prior to the encounter. When faced with a tough decision, such as that of taking the life of another, several factors will cloud your thinking; for example, your religious beliefs, or your fear of the consequences. Questions that must be asked are: Is the action necessary? Is the action justified? Can I live with the consequences? To determine if the action is necessary and justified, carefully reflect on the values you have inherited, weighing their merits and liabilities in the light of your own life, times, and circumstances. Determining the consequences of an action is often difficult and requires much analysis and reflection. But keep in mind that if faced with a high threat situation, where death is imminent, failing to be final may be a fatal mistake.

Most of us, when entering a martial arts program, choose to study for the purpose of self-defense. Other benefits, like building of confidence, physical fitness, tournament fighting, and social contacts may be equally important, but the main reason for taking self-defense is to learn how to defend ourselves. The general attitude is that violence and crime are common in our society, and that we run the risk of getting mugged, or robbed, or raped at least once in our lifetime. However, because of our upbringing or our religious beliefs, most of us live with a built in moral barrier that we are not willing to cross. This barrier keeps us from severely injuring or killing another person. Some even go so far as to say that killing is not justified under any circumstances, not even in self-defense. But the severity of a situation may dictate and change our moral barrier. If you have believed all your life that it is wrong to lie, when a stranger who is out to harm your best friend asks you where your friend is hiding, what will you do? In a situation like this, most of us would choose to tell a lie, because of our belief that a friend's life is more important than telling the truth. But some of us would not, because our moral barrier is too strong.

In the so called "no rules contests," where the fight continues until one person submits or is unable to go on, the "tap out" is a trusted and agreed upon way to end the fight without serious injury. But if there were truly no rules, and the fight was to the death, would you be able to move through your moral barrier and save your own life by seriously injuring your opponent? Does one person's gain have to be another's loss? Be honest with yourself when setting and accepting your moral barrier.

# When a Stand-Up Fighter Meets a Grappler

Although a fight could start on the ground, as if taken by surprise while in bed or at a campground, it will more likely start standing up, and then possibly go to the ground. If you are trained in the stand-up arts, you may feel tempted to fight with punches and kicks, even from the ground. If you are trained in the grappling arts, you will be more comfortable fighting from a position on the ground, relying on leverage and presses. Whether you are a stand-up fighter or a grappler, when practicing for takedowns, don't limit yourself to just one or the other. For example, you might start with a distraction that allows you to close distance or, if grabbed, use a finger lock to break the grip prior to your unbalancing move. If you manage to get behind your opponent and take him down with a rear choke, you most likely need to go to the ground with him in order to finish. Experiment with a partner and let him play the role of the stand-up fighter, while you play the role of the grappler. Your partner knows only how to strike and kick, while your goal is to get him on the ground and subdue him. If you are trained in the striking arts, you must now change your mind-set and think in terms of grappling. Try to close distance on your opponent and tie him up for a takedown. Try leg takedowns, tackles, and arm and neck takedowns. If you get in a clinch, try to get close enough to render your opponent's strikes harmless.

In most cases, a stand-up fighter has the advantage only prior to the clinch. Once the clinch happens, the stand-up fighter's strikes will do little damage, because he will have difficulty finding the leverage he needs to throw his strikes with power. If you are skilled at closing distance and manipulating balance, once you get in the clinch, the fight is basically over for the stand-up fighter, unless he is also schooled in the grappling arts and knows how to continue on the ground. For the purpose of this book, however, you should think in terms of self-defense and not sports. It is the unbalancing move itself that is your window of opportunity. Your goal is not to continue on the ground, unless you end up there unwillingly and there is no other possibility.

Now, let's assume that it is your opponent who is trying to clinch and unbalance you. When he reaches out to grab you, and it is evident that the fight will go to the ground, your first thought should be on leverage. It is leverage that gives you the mechanical advantage necessary to control a bigger adversary. Since your opponent is reaching for you, your focus will most likely be on his hands; they're the closest and most imminent threat. The elbow is a good point of leverage but, if going directly against the joint, ensure that your opponent's arm is straight. A bent arm gives your opponent more strength, because it is closer to his own center of mass. A bent arm presents no strain on his joint, and allows him to use muscular strength to defeat you. As discussed earlier, a bent arm must initially be defeated through the "crank" or the figure four lock.

Next, let's assume that you are already kneeling on the ground with your opponent. Take charge of the situation by timing your offense to his. When he reaches out to grab you, immediately move and intercept his arm. If you are a little out of reach, you can use straight arm balance manipulation by grabbing him in a cross wrist grab and pulling him toward you. If he is on his knees, he will have difficulty moving his foundation with the technique, and will therefore be off balance forward. Simultaneously pivot on your knees, until you have repositioned to the outside of his arm. Use your free hand against his elbow to straighten and control his arm. If done with intent, your opponent will end up on his stomach.

**When you have unbalanced your opponent, turn his elbow up and drop your knee onto his arm right above the elbow to immobilize the joint. Pull up on his wrist.**

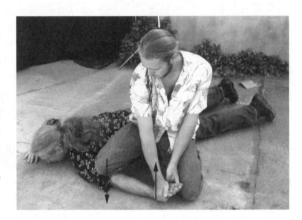

**An option is to sit on your opponent's head and shoulder to immobilize him, with his straight arm between your legs. Make sure that his elbow is pointed up. Pull his arm toward you, until it is in the vertical position. Keep your legs tight, and break the arm by pressing the elbow against your leg.**

# Getting Up from the Ground

Be aware of your stability when kneeling on the ground. Spread your legs slightly apart for a wider base, and rest on the balls of your feet (not the insteps). Resting on the balls of your feet allows you to get to a standing position quicker, while resting on the insteps may cause injury to your ankles if you are suddenly pushed off balance to the rear. Bend your upper body slightly at the waist. This lowers your center of gravity and limits frontal exposure to your opponent.

**If you have to kneel on the ground, assume a stance that affords you stability as well as mobility. Your hands can be planted for support when throwing a kick, and your knees can be used as pivot points.**

Note that lowering your butt slightly toward the ground increases the stability of the four-point stance. You may end up in a four-point stance when attempting to get up after a fall.

**If you get up like this, with your head low and your center of gravity high, your opponent can easily unbalance you with a kick.**

## Misaligning the Posture on the Ground

Taking an adversary down through neck manipulation from the four-point stance is identical in principle to the standing neck takedown. But because your opponent has much of his weight forward, unbalancing him to the rear is slightly more difficult. However, it is possible to take him straight back, if the technique is done with intent and preferably from a side position, where you are not working directly against his weight.

**Rear neck manipulation from the ground. If your opponent is in a sturdy four-point stance, this technique will not work as well.**

Fighting on the ground is very exhausting and requires strength. However, a small person may have an advantage over a larger adversary, if he knows how to use the leverage points on the human body to destroy his opponent's balance. The over and under, which is not a technique but a wrestling concept, may work well. Although you won't concern yourself with the rules of wrestling in a street confrontation, many of the concepts still hold true. The over and under simply means that in order to destroy your opponent's balance, you should place one arm over your first point of leverage, and the other arm under your second point of leverage, and use the push-pull principle (the half Nelson, for example).

**Think about this**

**The over and under helps you break your opponent's postural alignment, resulting in a loss of balance.**

The half Nelson from the kneeling position uses the over and under concept, and can be used to misalign your opponent's posture to the side. One of your arms comes under your opponent's armpit, with your hand over the back of his head. Use the push-pull principle to dip your opponent's shoulder toward the ground. When you have broken his postural alignment, it will only take minimal strength to manipulate his balance.

# A Final Reminder

My experiences as a student and instructor of martial arts tell me that if you only repeat back what others have taught you, you are not doing much to further your own skill. If your understanding is limited, you will not be able to adapt, and you will be ineffective in self-defense unless the situation happens exactly the way you have learned and practiced it. And what are the chances it will? It is impossible to foresee exactly how a situation will unfold. However, when you can analyze your own experiences and put together a system of self-defense that works for your particular physical build and mental attitude, it will bring insight beyond the boundaries of simple techniques. Understanding the concepts helps you avoid confusion at the time of the encounter. Techniques must therefore be generalized into broader patterns. A strike or grab to your wrist, waist, lapel, shoulder, or neck can be defended the same way, because the general pattern of the attack is identical. If a weapon (knife or stick) is involved, the only thing that changes is your timing, but the same principles still work. Many of these principles can also be used, with little modification at the beginning of a threat before you have been grabbed or hit, as well as the moment the threat materializes, and after you have been grabbed or hit.

Your goal when involved in a street encounter is to take your opponent to the ground and turn him to the inferior position, from where you can render him harmless. Because unbalancing moves are so much about leverage, the primary principle is to use the weight of your body when attempting to control your opponent. Maximum leverage comes from:

1. Keeping the technique in close proximity to your body. The farther a hold is from your center of mass, the more difficult it is to use your body weight. When you start to apply leverage, stay close to your opponent and allow your whole body weight to get involved in the technique.

2. Achieving a position of weakness in the target you are controlling. Don't apply strength against strength by going directly against the force. If controlling your opponent's arm, make sure it is turned so that you can go against the natural movement of the joint.

As soon as your opponent hits the ground or regains balance, he is likely to start fighting back. Try to rely on the multiple points of pain principle. This concept helps you split your opponent's focus, which, in turn, helps you execute your technique successfully, even against a stronger assailant. Use whatever tools you have available to create as many points of pain as possible. If movement or a hand change is needed, use your shoulders, knees, forearms, or point of chin to press your opponent's head, arms, or body to the ground.

Care should be taken to avoid becoming top heavy. Keep your center of gravity low to maintain your balance. A low center of gravity also gives your opponent fewer targets to attack. Don't get in a nearly unbalanced stance on the balls of both feet at the same time, unless your hands are also planted for stability. You can retain balance easier if at least one foot is flat against the ground. Be aware of where your feet are positioned, and of the location of your opponent's hands.

Use any object in the environment to your advantage. Just holding something in your hand is likely to increase your confidence. Many people don't think the home may be the most likely place for an attack to occur. How familiar are you with your home? What things in your home can be used as a weapon or press? When in your home, look around and pay attention to where these objects are located, and how to best utilize them in an encounter. What kinds of obstacles in your home can be used to help you unbalance an adversary? Couch, table, railing, stairs? Can you move so as to place your opponent with his back toward these obstacles? As you study these principles, note that there is an escape for every technique, and a knowledgeable opponent may be able to reverse the technique and use it against you. Be careful not to leave your arms or legs within easy reach of your opponent.

Based on the material discussed previously in this book, we will now look at a number of possible scenarios, and analyze what can be done in a similar situation, as well as what can go wrong, and possible ways to adapt.

## Scenario 1

You are involved in a verbal confrontation when the assailant approaches and reaches out to grab you. He gets hold of your shirtsleeve, but you pull your arm free. He takes a step forward and attempts a new grab. You know this person from earlier encounters, where he has yanked you off balance and down on the ground, and proceeded to kick you once or twice before leaving the scene.

**When the opponent grabs, pull free and time his next attempt to your unbalancing move.**

You use your knowledge of previous encounters to avoid the first grab attempt, and use it to time your opponent's next attempt. When he reaches out to grab you anew, you take advantage of his forward momentum and the fact that he has overextended his center of gravity slightly forward. You grab his wrist and move to the outside of his arm. You use your free arm to apply pressure behind the elbow of his extended arm, and start a circular rotation to unbalance him forward.

**Intercept your opponent's arm from a superior position to the side. Use the elbow as leverage, while driving forward with your body.**

There are several things that could happen from here. If you don't keep the technique close to your own center of mass, you risk losing control of your opponent. This may not necessarily be bad. If his momentum continues past you, for even a second or two, you may be in a position to get away. You may also be able to unbalance him, even if you lose your grip, by placing a hard front thrust kick to his lower back. This will at least buy you time.

Note that you can tighten the grip on your opponent's arm by overhooking his arm and encircling it a full 360 degrees, and pulling his arm tight to your body.

**If you lose the grip on your opponent's arm, a forceful thrust kick to the small of his back may accelerate his momentum away from you.**

Since you have been involved with this person in earlier encounters, it may be a good idea to consider how to keep this from happening again.

## Scenario 2

Now, let's say that you have intercepted your opponent's arm from the outside, but you fail to apply circular momentum. He resists the attack, and starts to turn toward you. You place a side kick into the natural bend of the back of his knee. This brings his upper body to the rear and starts an unbalancing move. You grab his head and continue pushing down, until he lands on his back. Help is nearby, so you drop a knee or shin press onto his head to control him.

**If you lose the grip, an attack against two points of balance: the head and the back of the knee can unbalance your opponent to the rear. When your intended defense fails, you must be prepared to adapt.**

It is important to understand that when a threat is real, you must become the aggressor rather than the victim. Roles must be reversed. Backpedaling in fear will fuel your opponent and make it nearly impossible for you to mount an effective defense. Experiment with your zone of safety on a partner. When should you start the unbalancing move, and when is it too late? If there is some distance between you and your adversary, you may have a chance to keep the attack from happening all together. If your opponent already has his arms wrapped around you, you may lose your window of opportunity and must create a new one. This delays your defense, prolongs the time during which you are endangered, and lessens your chances to succeed. Exactly how close should you allow your opponent to get before launching your counter-attack?

# Scenario 3

You have managed to take your attacker down. However, your escape routes are limited because of a wall behind you. In addition, a second attacker is emerging behind the first, and your first attacker is beginning to get back to his feet.

**If forced to deal with two attackers, try to keep at least one of them unbalanced at all times.**

Even a trained martial artist will find it difficult to fight two opponents simultaneously, so you must keep at least one of them in an unbalanced state. When the attacker on the ground starts to get up, you kick him forcefully off balance and into the second attacker. For this technique to work as intended, the timing must be so that the second attacker is within a few feet of the first when you execute your kick.

Now, let's say that the attacker on the ground is incapacitated and can't get up. You can now use him as a barrier between you and the second attacker. In order to reach you, the second attacker must either walk around the first attacker or step over him. If he walks around, he also gives you the opportunity to move in the opposite direction toward your escape route. If he steps over, he gives you the opportunity to use the attacker on the ground as a barrier to immobilize the second attacker's foundation for a forward unbalancing technique. Again, your technique must be correctly timed.

## Scenario 4

The attacker is empty handed, but is much bigger than you. You have managed to find a stick in the environment to use as an equalizer. When it is inevitable that you have to fight, you grab the stick horizontally with both hands and rush your opponent, forcing the stick against his upper body and throat in an attempt to unbalance him to the rear. The surprise of your attack, and the momentum, causes him to plunge backward into the wall behind him. You use the wall as a stabilizer for a press with the stick to his throat.

**A wall can be used in conjunction with a standing immobilization press. However, if up against a much bigger adversary, be aware of that his greater strength can defeat you.**

You rely on the no sensitivity principle of the stick; however, sometimes a technique that should have worked doesn't. Your opponent grabs the ends of the stick with both hands and, using his superior strength, pushes the stick and you away from him. When you realize that the technique is failing, your natural reaction is to struggle to reapply pressure. Your opponent twists the stick from your grip and throws you off balance. You must now find a new window of opportunity. Your opponent's defense has drained energy from you, and if you end up on the ground with him still standing, you are in a very bad position to continue. What would you do? Experiment with a partner to determine a course of action.

**When your opponent counters and starts to unbalance you, your natural reaction is to regain balance and control of the stick. But if you fight your opponent's point of attack, where his concerted strength and focus are, you are not likely to succeed.**

# Scenario 5

You have engaged your adversary for a neck takedown from the front. You grab his chin with one hand and the back of his head with the other for two points of balance, and try to tilt his head to the rear. But his neck is so strong that your technique has no effect. Your opponent reaches out with one hand, grabs you by the neck, slams you against a wall, and lifts you off your feet. **Caution: Don't try this neck lift in training. Be very careful when working with the neck.**

Your mind is now split and you are thinking more about your own balance than your opponent's. It is important to realize that sometimes the strength and size difference between two people is so great that knowledge of the principles is not enough to equalize the situation. Your hands will naturally go where the grip is. Once your opponent allows you to replant your feet, you might try to kick him hard to any target, and simultaneously grab any finger and bend it against its natural range of motion. The kick serves as a distraction for the finger hold, which will help lessen your opponent's grip. Continue with an unbalancing technique while your opponent's focus is split. If you can get him on the ground, it may afford you the opportunity to flee. The inertia of his heavier body is a disadvantage when he tries to get back to his feet.

# Scenario 6

We know that spreading out and keeping a low center of gravity brings stability. If you have studied grappling, you have probably learned how to pin your opponent to the ground by spreading your weight on top of him. Let's say that you have managed to get your much bigger opponent on his back, and that you are on top of him, covering his mouth and nose with your hand and pressing your forearm against his head to control him. You have lowered your center of gravity as much as possible to maintain stability, but your much stronger opponent grabs you with both hands and lifts you off of him.

**The press, or attempt to cut off the opponent's ability to breathe, is difficult when he is pushing you away. He can now easily throw you to the side.**

Although spreading your weight when pinning your opponent makes it difficult for him to throw you off, this is not a foolproof technique. A lightweight person is always at a disadvantage, no matter how good his technique is. You cannot increase your weight by spreading out; you can only increase your stability. If the scale says that you weigh 120 pounds, you weigh 120 pounds regardless of whether you keep a low or high center of gravity. If your opponent is able to bench press 120 pounds, he may simply place his hands on your ribs or hips and lift you straight up and off of him. This is why it is important to try to place your opponent in the inferior position on his stomach, where he has the least use of his hands. Preferably, his legs should also be flat against the ground, so that he can't use the leverage of a bent knee to push himself up.

Again, when you realize that the technique is failing, it is pointless to continue struggling with the same move. You will most likely be startled by the fact that your opponent is taking over the situation. If you can't get away and run, re-focus your attack on a different target. If your opponent throws you to the side in anger, try to roll with the momentum and get back to your feet. Because of your opponent's bigger mass, he requires more energy than you to get up from the ground. This may give you a window of opportunity to flee or proceed with a new unbalancing move. Note that a chaotic situation is difficult enough to deal with without the added stress of trying to keep your own balance. If your opponent has the opportunity to push you off balance, you won't have much of a chance.

# Scenario 7

You have been in an argument with your girlfriend. She is enraged and has managed to take you to the ground. You are on your back, and she is straddling you. She is holding you down with one hand and is getting ready to punch you with the other. You block her punching hand and simultaneously encircle her other arm with yours. Using the push-pull principle, you misalign her posture by pulling on the arm you have trapped, and pushing against her opposite shoulder. You also raise your hips off the ground and, as her butt comes up, reinforce her high center of gravity by kneeing her in the butt or small of back.

When she rolls off of you, you take advantage of her momentum by rolling with her to the top position. You end up between her legs in a slightly less favorable position than she was in earlier. You apply a forearm press to her jaw line.

If you are female with your male attacker on top of you, once you have reversed positions, you can use your elbows as a press against your opponent's inside thighs to push his legs apart. Grab his groin and squeeze hard. When your opponent reacts to the pain, try to get to your feet and escape.

Note that a heavy opponent can be pushed off of you easier if you join your center of gravity with his. You can now use his body momentum to your advantage. By pulling him close to you, he will become "one with you." When you raise your hips off the ground, keep your feet as wide as possible. A knowledgeable opponent may try to tie up your feet by pushing his feet against the outside of yours, narrowing your stance. Keeping your feet wide gives you more leverage when starting a circular motion to the side. Once your opponent starts losing balance, allow his heavier body to pull you along with him, until your positions are reversed. It is important to keep your arms bent throughout the technique, in order to keep the motion from exhausting itself through the opposing weight of your body.

# Scenario 8

Your opponent has lifted you off your feet in a bear hug from the front, and has both arms wrapped around your body. You place your hands on his chin and try to tilt his head to the rear to unbalance him. The technique is not working, so you kick your opponent's shins and knee him in the groin. The moment his focus splits, you grab his nose with one hand and pull up and back, while pushing with your other hand against his chin.

If this attack were done with your hands pinned, how would you proceed? Could you use your chin as a press against your opponent's sternum or face to split his focus? Could you still use your legs to kick? Your primary concern is to split his focus so that he frees at least one of your hands, and gives you a window of opportunity to unbalance him. What if he grabs you in a rear bear hug instead? If your hands are free, you can try to reach up behind you and grab his head and pull forward. If the distraction is enough to allow you to replant your feet, even if he doesn't let go of you, you can proceed with a forward throw by pushing your body back into his to join centers of gravity, and throwing him forward over your hip, using your grip on his neck for leverage.

**If your opponent has his arms wrapped around you, a forward throw using his neck as leverage may work. Remember to join centers of gravity, so that you won't be working against his greater weight.**

Let's say that your opponent grabs you around the neck from behind. When you feel the grip, you pull away and try to throw him. But it doesn't work, because there is a gap between your bodies, keeping you from joining centers of gravity with him. In order to throw a heavier adversary, you must first move your weight into him and replace his center of gravity with your own.

**If you pull away from your opponent, you won't be able to execute a throw.**

**Push your hips back into your opponent, and grab his fingers to break the grip. Or reach up and grab him around the neck for a forward throw.**

# Scenario 9

You observe your friend being unbalanced and attacked on the ground. The assailant is straddling your friend and threatening him with a knife. You look around for an object in the environment to be used as a weapon, but find none. The assailant's full focus is on attacking your friend. This gives you an opportunity to grab the assailant's chin from behind and forcefully tilt his head back, simultaneously pulling him off your friend.

**The fact that you are not the focus of this attack will work to your advantage. The attacker's full focus is on the person on the ground, making your rescue less expected, with a potentially good success rate.**

You might be able to strengthen this technique by kicking to your opponent's lower back or kidneys prior to or after grabbing his head. This would split his focus and bring his upper body back in the direction you are taking him. Once you have grabbed his chin, continue the rearward momentum by stepping back until your opponent is on the ground. Don't give him the opportunity to stand up and brace himself against your attack to his head.

Any object in the environment can strengthen your position and help you with the unbalancing technique. If you can't find a stick to be used as a striking weapon or for leverage, consider picking up a handful of dirt and rubbing it in your opponent's eyes just prior to unbalancing him. Do you have time to take your shirt off? Consider wrapping it over your opponent's head, or twisting it into a rope and placing it across his eyes, while pulling back forcefully.

**When your opponent can't see, he will have a hard time mounting an effective counter-attack against you.**

# Scenario 10

We often tend to define the attacker as male and the victim as female. But is it conceivable that a much smaller female would attack a much bigger male? Let's say that you are a man involved in a violent relationship, where your girlfriend kicks you in the groin and claws you across your face and back. You grab both of her arms and push her away from you. This only enrages her more, and she rushes you again. You yank her off balance, pin her arms to her body, and hold her until she calms down.

**Who is the victim here? A picture is not always worth a thousand words. You must have all the facts, before you can judge a situation.**

An acquaintance of mine was involved in a similar situation. The female sued, and the male, because he was male, and because of his much bigger size, had a hard time defending himself in court. Don't discount the not so obvious attacker. What if the little female had a knife? How would this negate your size and strength advantage?

Now that we have come to the end of the book, it is up to you to take what you have learned and explore on your own to determine which techniques and principles may help you in unrehearsed self-defense. The important part is that you find something that is suitable for your size, strength, and mental composure. I recommend getting together with somebody you know and trust to practice on a regular basis. Decide who is the attacker and who is the defender, and run through a number of situations in rapid succession, before trading roles. This will help you develop your ability to flow from one technique to the next, without having to think about it. Also, practice without determining who is the attacker and who is the defender, with the sole purpose of trying to be the first to get your partner on the ground.

# Final Thoughts

I'm sure you have heard the terms fighting spirit and killer instinct plenty of times. Although both terms may sound undesirable to the non-martial artist, when placed in their proper perspective, I'm convinced they are desirable qualities to have.

Fighting spirit is about controlling your body, mind, and spirit. But it is also about being in control of your body, mind, and spirit. It is about controlling what others are to do (or not do) with your body, mind, and spirit. Fighting spirit is about taking the active approach; it's about being the one who decides what, when, and how in issues that concern you.

Some people are more comfortable practicing martial techniques on a non-contact basis, but I don't believe fighting spirit can be developed this way. If you go to martial arts class and only practice kata (forms), or if you go to cardio-kickboxing class and throw a thousand punches and kicks, will you still be effective in a self-defense situation? My feelings are that there must be other people involved that you can test your body, mind, and spirit against.

Many people who abuse others don't really want to hurt them; they want to control them. You see this in all walks of life, and not just regarding physical contact. If you have fighting spirit, you control you. Period. What somebody else wants to do with you becomes irrelevant, because you are the higher authority on you. Having fighting spirit brings confidence and happiness and eradicates fear (the fear of victimization), and clears your mind to focus on the more positive aspects of life. When your mind is free, you know who you are and, as a result, you are more tolerant of others. You won't have a need anymore to force your beliefs or views on other people, it is not absolutely necessary that your spouse always agrees with you, and you can rejoice in other people's successes.

Whether in sports or in life, you cannot win without fighting spirit. Fighting spirit means not giving up; it means feeling a rush when stepping into the ring. I once jumped naked into the North Sea in 51 degree waters. Why? Because it's the body experience, it's like being pushed and shoved a little, it borders on pain without endangering your life. And I genuinely like that! I once volunteered to get pepper sprayed at the local police department, just to test my reaction and gain an understanding of myself. If you are uncomfortable with getting accidentally bumped by another customer when standing in line at the grocery store, my feelings are that you may have a little farther to go when developing real self-defense skills.

Some people's fighting spirit is so strong that they don't know when it's turning against them; they don't know when to quit in order to save themselves from severe injury. There are even times when your fighting spirit can result in your death. This is one reason we have referees and corner personnel to "throw in the towel." However, if I were in a street confrontation with nobody to throw in the towel for me, I would want this fighting spirit. I would rather get shot and killed on the spot than go with a stranger in his car. But this is me, and a conclusion I have come to after much thinking and analysis. You have to decide what is right for you, and hopefully after you have done a considerable amount of self-study.

I can think of a hundred other things to say about fighting spirit, but there is no doubt in my mind that it is something worthwhile to have.

**Reminder**  **Self-defense is not a technique; it's a mind-set. No weapon or skill can save you, if you lack the presence of mind to use it.**

# INDEX

## About the Author

Martina Sprague began her martial arts training in Aikido and Ed Parker's Kenpo karate in 1987, later finding an affinity for the full contact arts. She is a third degree black belt in kickboxing and modern freestyle. She is a flight instructor with a longstanding interest in aviation and the physical sciences. Her main focus in martial arts is on teaching and analyzing the concepts behind the techniques, and helping students apply the universal laws of physics to their particular style and physical and mental attributes.

Martina Sprague is an employee of Delta Air Lines. She lives and works in Salt Lake City, Utah.

**Also Available from Turtle Press:**

Fighting Science
Martial Arts Instructor's Desk Reference
Guide to Martial Arts Injury Care and Prevention
Solo Training
Fighter's Fact Book
Conceptual Self-defense
Martial Arts After 40
Warrior Speed
The Martial Arts Training Diary
The Martial Arts Training Diary for Kids
TeachingMartial Arts
Combat Strategy
The Art of Harmony
A Guide to Rape Awareness and Prevention
Total MindBody Training
1,001 Ways to Motivate Yourself and Others
Ultimate Fitness through Martial Arts
Weight Training for Martial Artists
A Part of the Ribbon: A Time Travel Adventure
Herding the Ox
Neng Da: Super Punches
Taekwondo Kyorugi: Olympic Style Sparring
Martial Arts for Women
Parents' Guide to Martial Arts
Strike Like Lightning: Meditations on Nature
Everyday Warriors

*For more information:*
*Turtle Press*
*PO Box 290206*
*Wethersfield CT 06129-206*
*1-800-77-TURTL*
*e-mail: sales@turtlepress.com*

*http://www.turtlepress.com*

DISCARD